"Here is a chronicle of ~~_____~~
of knowing that illness is a signal to change. The changes may involve nutrition and nurture, medications, jobs, relationships, spiritual awareness, and other dimensions of our lives. This book gives eloquent testimony to something I've learned over four decades of medical practice: When changes are made and healing comes; it is not just the patient who is changed but also the physician—and as Kristi Chrysler says so lovingly—a whole family as well."

Sidney M. Baker, MD FAAP, co-founder and
Medical Director Emeritus, Defeat Autism Now!

"Now that autism affects almost 1 in 67 families today, Kristi's book is an important read to overcome the ignorance surrounding autism and its far reaching effect on families. With accuracy and warmth, she depicts the stresses on marriage, finances, relationships, and mental health and offers hope in overcoming the desperate odds. May we be inspired to be sensitive to the needs of those affected around us individually and motivated collectively to ensure public policy that searches out the root causes of autism and addresses the pressing needs of hurting families."

Dave Weldon, U S Congressman

"This book is an inspirational story of one family's triumph over autism. Through her faith and trust in God, Kristi shows us all how to flourish under very difficult circumstances. We can all learn from her determination and deep-seated faith."

Dan Burton, US Congressman

"In this brutally honest story, you will find encouragement and wisdom that will have great meaning for your own life and marriage. Kristi Chrysler takes us on an amazing journey with her family through the valley of despair to a recovery and redemption that vividly portrays the faithfulness of God and the power of His truth in our lives."

James Muffett, founder Citizens
for Traditional Values

"As a mother, I am inspired by Kristi's dedication to her children and my respect for her as a mother is unparalleled. As a physician, I am inspired by her dedication to encourage all of us to follow our Spirit-guided pursuit of truth. We are blessed to have people like Kristi who show us the way to healing, even if it means helping us to learn new techniques and new methods of healing. I am happy to encourage doctors and health professionals throughout the country to never give up even when the diagnosis and prognosis seem overwhelming. This book from Kristi is a gift to all of us who care about our patients and seek to follow a non-traditional path of healing."

Tammy Born D.O., owner, Born
Preventative Health Care Clinic

"It was my privilege to share the good news of the Gospel with Kristi some years ago. She accepted the gift of eternal life with much joy. It has been exciting to watch Kristi grow in her faith as evidenced by her ability to overcome many difficulties in her life as explained in her book. She has been *a blessing to me as I walked through some deep waters. This book is an inspiration to all."*

Anne Kennedy, wife of Dr. D. James
Kennedy, Coral Ridge Ministries

"Poignant and poetic, Kristi's story begins where others end. A diagnosis of autism carries with it the prognosis of lifelong and forever and in that moment "Till Death Do Us Part" crashes on the shoals of finality.

Never has arrived. Caught between here and now there is no future. There is no family. There is only maintaining the moment; keeping your child safe while those around you talk of institutions and saying, "Goodbye," to the most precious gift the world can bestow.

How do you say, "Goodbye," to a three-year-old? You don't. You read Kristi's remarkable journey of Faith and Love. Love for her children, love for her husband, and finally love for herself as she makes her way out of one world, groping and terrified, and finds a better one. Nothing–no force, no fear, no despair can deny faith and love.

Kristi helpfully divides each chapter into major chords of purpose, finding fruit until the harvest of sustenance fills the soul and flows into the future riveting your mind and capturing your heart in Quixote moments of splendor. Far from tilting at windmills, Kristi slays the dragons of doubt to rise from the shoals and soar to the summit.

Kristi offers her life as a gift–her indomitable spirit to save all that is beautiful lights all of our lives. As a father of two boys with autism thank you for writing this book, Kristi."

Edmund C. Arranga, founder, Autism One

AUTISM

RECOVERY AGAINST ALL ODDS

AUTISM

RECOVERY AGAINST ALL ODDS

Kristi Chrysler

TATE PUBLISHING & *Enterprises*

Published by Tate Publishing & Enterprises, LLC
127 E. Trade Center Terrace | Mustang, Oklahoma 73064 USA
1.888.361.9473 | www.tatepublishing.com

Tate Publishing is committed to excellence in the publishing industry. The company reflects the philosophy established by the founders, based on Psalm 68:11,
"The Lord gave the word and great was the company of those who published it."

Book design copyright © 2007 by Tate Publishing, LLC. All rights reserved.
Cover design by Lynly D. Taylor
Interior design by Isaiah R. McKee

Published in the United States of America

ISBN: 978-1-60462-274-4
1. Family and Relationships: Children with Special Needs/Parenting
2. Psychology: Behavior Therapy

08.02.08

This book is dedicated to my family, without them there would be no story to share. To the late Dr. Kennedy and his wife, Anne, for their investment in my salvation and walk with the Lord. And to Christ, without Him I would not have had the strength to endure this race.

Ultimately this book is dedicated to the many families and children still suffering with autism. It is for you that I have been inspired to share our story to encourage you to run this race, as so many did for me and saw us through to the finish line.

ACKNOWLEDGMENTS

I must deeply thank my children, Chloe, Heather, Richie, John, and Kyle for their support, encouragement, and continual prayers for me in writing this book. Without their extra efforts in so many areas and love it would not have been possible to achieve Richie's recovery or write this book. To Rick for his encouragement for me to write and his technical assistance. To my parents, Jack and Sherry, who through their life and love gave me the encouragement to endure. To my many friends who lent their input, prayers, support, and encouragement: Jeannie, Anne, Amy, Pamela, Nancy, Susan, Sandy, Becca, Lori, Twyla, Abigail, and all the LIGHT Ministry Moms. To Nancy and Hank for their home to write. And to many others who prayed for this project. To David Hancock and Wes Taylor for their inspiration and encouragement, which birthed this book. To Dr. Sidney Baker and in remembrance of Bernie Rimland Ph.D., who co-founded Defeat Autism Now!, our turning point for hope. Dr. Jeff Bradstreet, who saw us into recovery and maintenance. To all those at Tate Publishing, Tracy Terrell, my encouraging editor, and especially Dr. Richard Tate, whose encouragement given from the start inspired me to complete this project.

Finally, to my Lord Jesus, who gave me every detail I needed to accomplish this book—I owe everything to You.

TABLE OF CONTENTS

FOREWORD

Autism is not a simplistic condition. At the biological level, it delays or completely derails normal language development, while inducing odd repetitive behaviors and social withdrawal. Once thought to be purely a genetic disorder, there is now growing consensus that autism represents an extraordinarily complex interaction of genetics with environmental effects, including any number of toxins, viruses, and bacteria.

Richie's story is like that of many children I have known over the past ten years of my medical career. His has its own unique features, trials, setbacks, and victories, but his battle stands as yet another testimonial to the fact that autism is not always a life-long condition. Children can recover. As Richie's parents set out to rebuild his lagging development with determination, hope, and persistence, they anchored their quest to the rock of faith in God's unfailing love.

At a recent retreat where autism experts from around the world met to discuss the key elements underpinning the cases of successful restoration and recovery, one factor kept reoccurring as a theme: parental persistence. Perhaps not so surprisingly, experts from biochemistry to psychology and gastroenterology to immunology all agreed that it was the steadfast parents who stayed on course and withstood, sometimes, years of failures who held the best chances of seeing tremendous gains in their children's developmental progress.

So if you are a parent, what are the things you must persistently pursue? First, you must recognize you are your child's main advocate. No one will go to bat for your kid like you—no one. No educator, no doctor, no therapist could ever match your dedication to your child. But there is more; you must be persistent in making goals and coordinating plans to see to it those goals are met or reconsidered frequently. But how do you know what to do, who to trust, where to find reliable information? These are daily challenges we all face as we try to parent and care for our sons and daughters. I, too, am a parent of a boy with autism—an awesome young man who has regained much of what was lost during his regressive phases from seizures, bowel disease, and other problems. Even as a medical doctor working full-time in this field, knowing which therapies to budget for remains problematic.

And budget is more than just money. There is also the time budget. Some things, like applied behavioral analysis therapy (ABA), are both costly and time consuming, but ABA is also the best documented pathway to recovery. Other interventions are as simple sounding as giving a vitamin pill once a day, that is until you actually try giving a child with a heightened gag reflex, sensory dysfunction, and gut inflammation vitamins or fish oil or even regular food. Suddenly, what should be this simple process requires consultation with oral-motor therapist and behavioral analysts. Somehow you have to know this is important enough to keep at it, even when it seems impossible.

So where does that inner strength come from? For many of the families I know and for me as well, it came from jumping in without concern that the water is likely over your head. You will learn to swim; you have no choice because the alternative of abandoning your child to the land of autism is just not an option you can sleep with. Jumping in means finding parents like Kristi or support groups of parents that are doing it successfully and the right chat room on the Web. Finding the right parent forum on the Web is very challenging. Emotions run high in this battle. Opinions about current in vogue treatment options seem to take on religious zeal despite an absence of objective or control studies to support that particular intervention. Yet, waiting for the university-based, double-blind controlled study seems like an impossibly distant option that will let your child's chances slip away, as the years of waiting pass without much help coming from our main institutions: government, medical schools, and professional academies.

The approach Kristi describes in *Autism: Recovery Against All Odds* is one of blending faith, behavioral strategies, and therapies (meaning lots of one-on-one time) with biomedical interventions. The latter of these is clearly the most controversial and challenging to sort out. The biomedical spectrum of autism interventions parents most sort through runs from restricted diets to heavy metal detoxification (often called chelation). It also spans widely disparate approaches, such as homeopathy and intravenous immune therapy with purified human antibodies. And all of it has some level of documentation and support in either the medical literature or books written by doctors and parents to document varying degrees of success.

You must also persist in the midst of failure. Each child is unique. What helps one child in the recovery process may actually hinder another. Prioritize your child's needs, and you will get a better starting place. For example, when a child with diarrhea and eczema has an outrageous, seemingly addictive need for milk, you are pretty much assured you will see remarkable gains in behavior and sleep by removing milk. This type of wisdom is shared on Web sites about various diets and autism, as well as the now numerous, high-quality autism biomedical type conferences.

Throughout this process, parents battle their own personal challenges. Kristi bravely tells her own story, even her own personal health issues, but the ultimate blessings of every challenge come from the powerful lessons of faith and grace they teach. Every family battling autism is at high risk. The process of loss of normalcy, expensive therapies, the need for hypervigilance to protect the child from harm, the lack of sleep, the long list of associated medical problems all combine to fatigue the strongest bonds and erode personal relationships. This process strains siblings in complex ways, yet parents often have little time or energy left to help the other family members.

In the end, without a solid grounding in personal strength and faith in God it is hard to imagine surviving the battle. Yet with these I see both children and their parents thrive in the face of what would otherwise be insurmountable odds.

Jeffrey Bradstreet, M.D. F.A.A.F.P.
Director of the International Child Development and
Resource Center

INTRODUCTION

Considering writing this book took me into great amounts of prayer and reflection, since my life seemed too busy to consider such a feat. While attending a writer's conference with my oldest daughter, hoping to develop her abilities and help me gain insight into completing a children's series of books I had begun writing years ago, one interactive speaker changed my focus and allowed God to show me His desires. During a workshop we were given an assignment to take a subject from life experience and quickly write down six to twelve topics regarding that subject. Well, for me it was a given—autism. Not long before this conference would I have even dreamed it possible to leave my four younger children for a long weekend to attend such a conference, due to one of them having autism. Since his recent recovery, this was my first outing alone, without him, without worry.

I quickly completed the assignment given and was then called upon to share my writings out loud. After sharing I was asked many questions regarding the subject of recovering my child from autism. The speaker happened to be a New York publisher and his top editor recently had his own child diagnosed with autism, which sparked his interest to hear that recovery from autism was possible. This interactive conversation led to many people from the conference approaching me after class with questions about my son's recovery, since they, too, *knew* of someone who was battling autism. After much prayer I realized that this was the direction my writing needed to focus on, and I needed to tell our story to encourage and help others come out of the darkness of autism and into the light.

I am so very grateful for all the many ways the Lord

has carried us through the dark and stormy days dealing with autism as well as other challenges in life. But I have to admit, I battled the thought of writing this book. I came up with many good reasons not to write it at all or many reasons just to wait. From having to relive extremely painful experiences to protecting my family and children's privacy, I justified this was not the right timing. But, after seeking the Lord, I felt He was leading me in this way, and my husband also encouraged and supported the idea. I still put tackling this endeavor off. Life was so busy. Then one day I attended a Revive Our Hearts woman's conference by Nancy Leigh DeMoss and there totally surrendered control with the writing of this book to God. Although I am often up for a challenge, it truly took the hand of God through that conference along with others who continued to draw out of me all the insights I have learned that I realized I need not wait to get the awareness out, since autism is such an epidemic leaving children, marriages, and families left behind like the aftermath of a hurricane. Autism is treatable and even reversible in many cases, and most importantly, families can be spared devastating effects during the process. As Nancy Leigh DeMoss writes in her book, *Surrender,*

> If we do not trust God's promises and, therefore, do not step out in faith and surrender, we will ultimately find ourselves in bondage to the very things we refuse to surrender. We will end up being controlled by that which we are seeking to keep within our own control.[1]

My desires have always been to help others. And I would never shy from sharing with another family or friends I met at a small group meeting all the insights I had gained. This project, however, went far beyond anything I felt ready to embark upon with my continuing demanding schedule of homeschooling five children and helping my husband with business, trying to recoup our lost finances during the pursuit of recovering our son, busy serving in ministry, thus why this book has been accomplished through the Lord's strength, once again, and not of my own. I just couldn't get past the feeling that perhaps someone could be helped from the information contained in the following pages. If even one parent is encouraged, one child is helped, or one marriage is given hope, the sacrifice and time invested will be worth it for me, just as the sacrifice of five years of intense work was to bring my son to recovery. I continue to share with other families that it's really such a short time of commitment for his lifetime (and ours) of gain. Our family has been given new hope, new joy, truly a new life. Without a doubt, I would do it again if I had to.

In following the Lord's leading with the writing of this book from its inception recollects a story I once heard. A man was walking down the shoreline of the ocean after the tide had washed out to sea. As he did, there were left on the shore thousands of starfish that had washed up and were now stranded. Every few steps the man would bend down and pick up a little starfish, toss it back into the water, and then continue to walk a few steps, bend down, pick up another starfish, and toss it back into the ocean. As he continued in this way a jogger was approaching toward him and observed what this man was doing. Thinking he must be a crazy old fool, he stopped and questioned the old man, "Why are you bothering to stop and throw any of these starfish back into the water? There are thousands; they're everywhere. You can't possibly hope to make a difference in what you're doing."

The old man had listened intently to this young jogger, then bent down, picked up another starfish, tossed it back into the ocean and replied, "It made a difference to that one."

That is a reminder to me of perhaps why I wrote this book. If it makes a difference to even one—child, mother, or marriage—it makes a difference.

It is my desire that this book not be an exploitation of anything short of the hand of God in the life of our family to inspire and encourage others to turn to the Lord when hit with heavy burdens of life. All the glory of recovery for my son ultimately goes to Him, for without Him nothing that was accomplished could have been. It is truly through my gratitude of my faith in Jesus Christ that I feel I ever had a chance to survive the destruction that could have come to my family while dealing with the awesome task of altering the course autism was making.

Recovery

It's interesting to note Webster's definition for recovery:

1. Return to an original state.
2. Gradual healing (through rest) after sickness or injury.

3. The act of regaining or saving something lost (or in danger of becoming lost).

    That's exactly what I longed for with our son. Prior to his regression into autism, he was a sweet, lovable babbling baby. My desire was to "return him to his original state." It was through gradual healing. And I do feel we were regaining or saving something that was lost—our son.

    Recovery is possible. To what degree for each person, I don't know. Each child is unique, especially in the world of autism. Every family has different dynamics that make it peculiar and special. But I believe with my heart that each family and extended family can have autism actually play a role of relinquishing the love within while acquiring attributes that refine us to conform to the image of Christ. And any positive results on the road to recovery will be such a bonus! It's really up to each individual. Autism doesn't have to bring us down; instead, as it and many other challenges in life have taught me, we can allow autism to mold us into people of greater character, integrity, and servant hood. That's really what life is about, serving others while glorifying God. Autism is just a vehicle to teach those of us who deal with this disorder how to better give of ourselves and put others needs before our own by reaching into another world and thinking on that which is pure, lovely, and true. This is done not only through the parents of a child battling autism, but through friends, family, and those who work with these children. The results experienced in the end will be worth every ounce of sacrifice given. Reflecting on the fact that a pearl would never become the lovely lustrous beauty it is without the gnawing of sand inside the shell of the clam it lives in reminds me of how autism can produce that pearl within every child, parent, and family it inflicts—like the sand—we just have to allow it to polish us rather than destroy us.

I turn often to my Bible for direction in life. In God's Word we read, "And the words of the LORD are flawless, like silver refined in a furnace of clay, purified seven times" (Psalms 12:6). In a daily devotional by Joni Erickson Tada and Friends, I appreciate the insight shared into this verse,

> One unusual quality of silver that accentuates its purity is the ability it has to kill bacteria when it comes in contact with it. It's as if "bad things" can't survive in silver, or around it! So, too, the Word of God is not only pure in and of itself, it has the ability, when applied by faith, to cleanse the reader of his or her sin. God is not as concerned about people finding his words "golden," all beautiful and attractive, as he is in people's lives being touched by the 'silver' of his word— becoming changed, holy, and pure.[2]

That's why, I believe we need to seek God's Word and allow autism to refine us—developing that pearl within us. In I Corinthians 13:3 it says, "And now abide in faith, hope, love, these three; but the greatest of these is love" (NKJV). No matter what state our child is in, the greatest gift we can give is love.

Whether autism inflicts your own child, a patient, friend, or family member, you can play an important role in their life and not only benefit a deserving child, but benefit yourself in the process. Become a person of influence. Develop the pearl within others who are enduring life's struggles.

"Bear one another's burdens, and so fulfill the law of Christ" (Galatians 6:2).

FAMILY BEGINNINGS

Faithfulness:
"Now faith is the substance of things hoped for,
the evidence of things not seen." Hebrews 11:1

Our Beginning

As with many young women I dreamed often about one day meeting Mr. Wonderful, marrying him, and having a family. I longed often to cuddle a little baby in my arms and experience that miracle of life. Then I would live happily ever after. My hope for that kind of marriage and family life began to fade shortly after the birth of our first child.

As excited as I was about finding out I was pregnant just six months after we were married, I quickly realized that my husband was counting on a little more time for *just the two of us.* Marriage for us happened quickly. We met and were married just six months later! It was a blessing to have Rick working from home during that time so our first year and a half of marriage was spent almost twenty-four hours a day together—growing, working, and enjoying our sweet time of total togetherness.

Then our first daughter was born healthy and strong. Nothing short of a precious miracle, as I recall the amazing bond I felt immediately upon holding her. But that quickly changed, as she soon developed day and night screaming bouts that lasted for hours. She couldn't ride in a car seat or sleep in a crib, since intense screaming would produce vomiting, and if she wasn't completely upright she would begin to aspirate. I quickly learned how to clear her airway when this did happen. Those brief days of looking into her sweet eyes, experiencing that love bond were wiped out by the exhausting times of caring for her, making sure that she didn't aspirate during her nonstop screaming.

Our fears increased when doctors thought she had a

tumor causing all the pain and hardness in her abdomen. But after testing, her diagnosis resulted in "severe colic." Relieved that we weren't dealing with a tumor, we now had no hope in relieving her pain and the accompanying screaming, according to doctors. We would simply have to wait until she outgrew it. So my happily-ever-after dream began to give glimpses to the reality of life. I began to finally understand how a lonely, single mom could abandon a little helpless infant in some garbage can, as I had often heard was happening in the city news. Severe colic coupled with after-birth recovery and sleepless exhaustion produces such emotional turmoil within a mother's heart that I found myself extremely grateful for family support and bumpy, dirt roads. (She would drift off for moments of sleep while I held her driving on dirt roads!) I was also fortunate to have a father-in-law training for a triathlon so he would hold her and work out for hours on the treadmill, stair climber, and stationary bike using endurance that her severe colic had robbed the rest of us of. She seemed settled during these times and this gave us little breaks. My parents were also a great support, helping in every way they could, bringing meals, doing our laundry, and having us over during these trying days. I was so grateful for each person's help.

How sad I was, though, when my hopes and dreams seemed to be shattering through the growth of our first young child. Our total togetherness my husband and I had once experienced was quickly replaced with total focus on our sick little baby. We didn't enjoy anything like most new parents did. We couldn't go for walks; she needed to be bounced. The beautiful brass crib sat unattended. I tried going to Gymboree and even joined a play group to meet other moms, since we had moved from Michigan to Florida when she was two months old. But in each case I would find myself in a corner with a screaming infant, stares, and those judgmental looks flying my way, as I held, bounced, and comforted my little girl, but usually to no avail. I even recall times when trying to grocery shop other "older and wiser women" would come up to me and tell me how I should go home and feed my starving baby before coming shopping. Little did they know she had just eaten and the food was likely the cause of her severe stomach pain. When I tried to explain she had severe colic, they would scuffle away with those judgmental stares as if I were a new mom who wasn't caring for my new baby. How defeated and isolated I often felt.

She finally outgrew the colic around eight months of age, but I found myself not recovering very well. I thought I just needed to catch up on all those months of sleepless nights, but I began having a series of unusual symptoms from extreme fatigue and lethargy to numbness and pain throughout my bones and joints, along with severe mouth ulcers that prevented me to eat. I had a hard time functioning, and normal daily activities would wear me to exhaustion. I felt like a failure since I couldn't seem to keep up with life.

After many tests and many negative results, I found myself trying to pull out of *it,* whatever *it* was, and get my energy back to be a productive wife and mother. Every day, however, seemed a struggle. When our daughter was two, I found myself pregnant once more. I was excited again! All those old hopes and dreams surfaced once more to cuddle and hold a sweet baby. I thought maybe this time would be different. But my pregnancy quickly turned sour as I became very, very ill. I lost ten pounds during my first four months pregnant, and we all became concerned. I ended up with pre-term labor and on bed rest from about my sixth month on. This was a new and exciting challenge to have a toddler and be on bed rest.

But the blessing was that our colicky screaming baby developed into a little two-year-old—a sweet, loving, and caring young toddler and we never experienced anything *terrible* during those years with her. We decided that she used up all her energy during those long colicky months so we were blessed during her toddler years!

Now on bed rest, I had made a game of it for her to *play mommy* and get me items I needed as we spent our days playing in bed together. I've learned that every challenge must be taken as an adventure to keep the right attitude and allow it to develop the good and not the bad within you. It's always a choice to grow bitter and wallow in self-pity or to deal with what life has presented you the best you can. I always found since I didn't have a choice in the matters of life, I best figure out a way to deal with it positively. But those attitudes didn't just emerge within me. I spent many hours reading God's Word and devotionals, listening to sermons and reading books on proper attitudes that helped me gain continual perspective with my situation at hand. I found that having a child by my side, I needed to make a game of finding something positive with our situation. I have found that by doing this in every aspect of life we will be well equipped to persevere with the right attitude and to pass that attitude on to those around us. God is sovereign and makes no mistakes, even when we do. I do believe He allows whatever happens in our life to conform us closer to the image of His Son. Although it's taken me much prayer to accept this fact, since I have I am better able to accept daily difficulties as a character-building moments.

It was an exciting time in life, we had moved back to Michigan just prior to my bed rest restrictions and into our old home, which was also the headquarters of my father-in-law's congressional campaign. The location and layout of the home made it an ideal fit for the beginning stages of this second campaign for U.S. Congress to launch its efforts. So, though I was on continual bed rest you might say it never got dull or too quiet as the phone ringing, faxes, and people coming and going gave a unique flare to "bed rest" (and privacy, I might add) as I worked hard to allow this new baby developing grow to a safe weight and age before birth.

Our second daughter was born just slightly early and without any complications, despite her many attempts at upping her due date. But this time I became very ill after her birth. It was much worse than before. After additional testing I was diagnosed with Systemic Lupus Erythematosus (SLE) an auto-immune disease in which my immune system was confused and worked overtime attacking my own body. I ended up on about nine medications and very ill. In continual pain and unable to walk very well at times, I even fell once going down the stairs while carrying our new daughter and accidentally broke her leg and my vertebrae. The disease was progressing rapidly as I began to experience issues with my lungs and heart, at times being rushed off to the hospital. Although I was on so much medication, it didn't seem to be making me feel much better or altering the course of the disease.

It seemed there must be another answer. I never liked taking medications to counteract the side effects of the other medications I took. But the vicious cycle I was on trying to cope with the intense pain and disabling effects Lupus was inflicting on my life kept me searching for relief. So, I set out to search for other options. Diet and nutrition seemed to be the area of greatest hope. After learning all I could, I began to make major changes in what I ate along with adding supplements and herbs into my diet. We even learned how to grind our own wheat, make flour and fresh bread, shop organic, and enjoy "whole foods." I finally began to experience relief in many areas.

Desiring another baby (and hoping to carry on our family name with a boy) these natural remedies soon allowed me to get off all the medications and actually begin an adequate remission from the disease so we could entertain that conversation of expanding our family. I wasn't symptom free, but I could manage without heavy doses of medications. Although my rheumatologist was not favorable, my desire for another baby outweighed his caution and he agreed if I was seen in the high-risk pregnancy clinic. I soon learned how to control the disease naturally and maintained a state of remission, so then pregnancy became an option once again. I was feeling better than I had in years, and I was finally really enjoying life with my young family for the first time. Rick decided to join his father (now a U.S. Congressman and up for re-election) in service to our community by running for County Commissioner. Having gained much insight with work from all of his father's campaigns, he asked that I become his campaign manager and we began rekindling the fun times of spending lots of time together strategizing, working, and enjoying our family.

During this season I became pregnant but it ended in a miscarriage. Shortly after, we found I was pregnant again. Cautiously proceeding, I took great measures to care for this baby. But again, another miscarriage and the emotions that go with one loss after another. After so many people questioned me, especially at church, I began to wonder why I was experiencing so many hardships. Why everything seemed to happen the hard way. But, I couldn't allow myself to wallow in wondering; we were just too busy. I had begun to read and listen to tapes during my bed rest days and those insights gained during that time proved inspirational as life continued to offer many mountains to hurdle. God's Word was the cornerstone for me, but I also gained much insight from sermons and motivational speakers as well. I've found that it's so important to have continual positive input in my life to keep my thoughts balanced when those inevitable challenges arise. And I continue to read and listen to anything that will direct me upward through inward examinations and changes of my own attitude. It's something I've found that needs continual maintenance.

After dealing with the second baby lost, I learned that due to having lupus, I could be susceptible to miscarriages. It's not that I couldn't have another baby; I just had to be seen and treated as a "high-risk" pregnancy patient. Soon I was pregnant once again, and this time we learned and did all we could to help this pregnancy go full term. I was on and off bed rest again and learned of many natural ways to help this baby grow healthy, which allowed this pregnancy to succeed. Due on Christmas Day, I went into labor on Thanksgiving Day; our son was born, and we all rejoiced in God's provision.

After our son was born, I soon found myself pregnant again. Getting pregnant didn't seem to be a challenge I faced and many had fun teasing Rick and me about that. But keeping up with the babies, miscarriages, and my own health was a bit more challenging. This pregnancy seemed different. I became very ill again. And we were concerned about the pregnancy repeating scenes from my second pregnancy. Wondering if somehow I was slipping out of remission from the lupus, we searched for answers. Soon we learned that this was not a normal pregnancy and that was why I was so sick. This was a molar pregnancy, where a mass of tissue develops that can become cancerous.

I needed surgery to remove and biopsy the mass. With three young children I went in for the first surgery I had ever had, not knowing whether I would face cancer or not. The biopsy was negative but then came the next news. The mass could quickly grow back and if it did, would likely be cancerous. Thus, I needed to go in for weekly blood tests, meet with oncologists, and be sure not to get pregnant for at least four months. So, that was life for the next few months—with an infant, two and five year old, traipsing off to the hospital lab weekly having blood drawn, and then awaiting the call for the results. It was like being on pins and needles all the time. I couldn't try to forget about it because it was ever before me. It was at this time that my faith in the Lord became more and more important to me, trusting Him with whatever might happen to me. Knowing that if I did get this cancer I might not be there to raise three young children, and my dear husband was hardly ready to take on that task alone. He was still adjusting to our family expanding. I was grateful to have had a mother who had survived serious cancer, non-Hodgkin's lymphoma, which helped me recognize that cancer could be defeated. However, being there with my mother in my early twenties, assisting her during her battle, and knowing firsthand the toll it took on our lives, I couldn't conceive how I could possibly succeed the way she did having such young children.

Faith, prayer, friends, and family were my support during those days. Realizing that my life was but a vapor, and I needed to make the most of each day I had kept my focus channeled. I knew I had to relinquish any control I tried to have over it to God, who was the only one in control. It was at the end of the third month that I began to experience symptoms of pregnancy. We were trying to avoid pregnancy so the scare was prevalent that the mass had returned, masking itself as another pregnancy and this time would likely be cancerous. Our prayers increased as our anxieties heightened, while trying to give everything over to the Lord.

But test results revealed another healthy-looking pregnancy! What joy and relief we felt. Although we missed waiting the additional month, doctors felt we were safe at that point to carry on with this pregnancy. The pregnancy went well, and soon we had another baby boy. Life was full and busy—a newborn, one-year-old, three-year-old, and five-year-old. Although I did begin to experience some symptoms of lupus, I continued to eat and live as healthy a life as I could and just push past the symptoms and pain to maintain my daily routine of a busy family.

Throughout this time of our growing family, my husband and I, along with his family were busy in business and politics. We had been through one successful campaign for him, where he served two years, and were upcoming another campaign. We enjoyed working together on all of his campaigns, as well as those for his father, and all the children joined us in attending functions, visiting people, passing out literature, being in parades, and singing at events. The first time my children went to *see* a parade they thought something was wrong since they weren't *walking* in it and instead were just spectators on the sidelines! That's how they were growing up. Involved, active, and serving. We so loved to serve in our community together as a family through church and political service. Rick was a dedicated official and very committed to serving the people well. But this busy political life did take him away from our growing family many evenings due to meetings and functions that we couldn't all attend.

Additional Challenges

While I was pregnant with our fourth child, all three of our other children were exposed and came down with the chicken pox the very same day. Everything started out normal, until three days into the virus our oldest daughter, who was five at that time, was unable to walk or talk. We rushed her to the doctor, and they quickly

evaluated her and consulted the pediatric neural specialist at the University Children's Hospital, who diagnosed
her with cerebellar ataxia—the rare side effect from the
chicken pox virus that no one, except the pediatric neurologist, ever seemed to hear of anyone getting. It caused
her to have symptoms as if she had a closed head injury.
Even her sweet-natured personality changed to aggressive and mean behavior. She wore a helmet to protect her
from further injury as she staggered trying to walk. She
killed bugs, hit, screamed, was just plain mean and often
uncontrollable. She wasn't our daughter at all. The sever-
ity lasted for about four weeks. Our prayer by that time
was just that she regain her sweet personality, even if she
could never walk or talk the same again. We were grateful to our church, friends, and family who joined us in
prayer as her personality resurfaced and we began to get
our sweet little girl back. In time, she was able to walk
and talk. However, she lost much of her memory and
had to relearn how to read, write, and she experienced
many additional challenges with balance and processing
thoughts. Since I had been the one to teach her at home
through homeschooling, we went back and sought to
reteach everything. This was a time to just focus on the
gratitude that she did regain her sweet personality—yet
her quick and easy ability to learn had been replaced with
many struggles and learning disabilities, which proved
challenging for both of us.

Right after the birth of our fourth son, Rick seriously
talked with me about the fact that our family was growing at such a quick rate. Although he told me he loved
each time I was pregnant and was happy with me as a
wife and mother, he had concerns for my health, which

continued to be a struggle for me. His concerns were well validated as I continued to battle bouts of lupus flares likely due to many sleepless nights with raising our young children. We were in the midst of discussions on the subject and what we would do when I learned that I was once again pregnant! I was afraid to even tell Rick, as we were still in the midst of discussions evaluating my health and since I knew his concerns for our growing family and the doctors were sharing his concerns for my health as well. I thought this news would be difficult for him to receive.

As always, despite the previous conversations, he received the news well, and with love, support, and anticipation we proceeded through another pregnancy. Other than developing a blot clot that led to intermittent times of bed rest and restricted activity (just another character-building time in life juggling that with now having four young children) our fifth child was born without complications. By this time I had learned to eat carefully to avoid major bouts of colic with a newborn, since all five of our children suffered with stomach issues and this also helped me keep the lupus flares in check during the newborn's sleepless nights.

However, amidst our growing family and the excitement of a new baby, something didn't seem right. There was an unusual amount of heightened stress and fragmentation. I thought it must be our very quick, young, and growing family. I began to feel inapt at handling so many children. But I observed friends who had even more children than I did, and they were all going places and doing well. So I began to seek out advice on what I was doing wrong. Many a friend shared with me disciplining ideas, training tips, organizing tips, books from the experts—you name it, I got it. But hard as I tried, life continued to get more and more harried. I began to feel isolated and alone. I couldn't go much of anywhere due to behaviors with my three young boys that were beginning to become beyond alarming. I felt like most people didn't want to bring their children to my home, due to the growing aggression coupled with odd behaviors, especially developing within our oldest son, Richie.

I sought out the advice of a pediatrician who conceded that I must be expecting too much of my three young boys since I was used to a girl's rate of maturity, raising two girls first. I would later learn that this was often communicated to many parents when first seeking a physician's input on the questionable behavioral issues in their child. I am grateful that with all the work of advocates for autism, awareness and detection for early diagnosis is much easier to come by than it was when our son was young and experiencing beginning symptoms.

For me, I began to wonder, if it wasn't my boys then—what was *my* problem? Why couldn't *I* handle boys? What was wrong with *me?* Those became my daily haunting questions as I slipped deeper into a reality that something must be wrong and if it wasn't my boys, then it must be me. I certainly faced enough judgmental looks and comments just having a larger family. Adding bizarre behavior to it didn't help. So I set out to be more consistent than anyone else. I had read that 99% consistency in child training would amount to an untrained child, and with the behaviors we faced moment by moment daily, I knew I must be missing the mark. I would set out being

100% consistent in every area with them. That must be the ticket.

REFLECTIONS FOR RECOVERY

∞ Have you had dreams of marriage and family life that haven't measured up to your imaginations? If so, take each situation and view it as a "character builder," rather than allowing it to bring you down or even destroy you.

∞ Where do you turn when you are feeling defeated with your children? With your marriage? Be sure you turn to God first. Guard yourself against negative, critical people. Take the words or advice they are giving but leave the negative emotion behind. It's always a choice what we receive and what we deflect.

∞ Turning to God alone is the best place to go. Do you have a personal relationship with God? Have you confessed your own sin and unworthiness and accepted His free and waiting gift of eternal life given just for you? If not, consider praying right now and asking Christ to come into your life and make it new. For me, that made all the difference in my attitude and acceptance of challenging situations. Knowing I could go to a gracious God who was always available to me, always accessible to gain strength, was ultimately what kept me from going in the wrong direction during many trying times.

∞ Are you willing to keep trying, no matter what the cost, to keep in line with God's Word and be a person of integrity? Ask yourself the question and then decide if becoming a person of character and integrity is your desire, no matter what the cost.

∞ Reminding myself daily of the suffering that Christ did on my behalf helped me keep in perspective the ways I felt I was suffering. When life didn't seem fair, I could reflect on the absolute unfairness Christ endured by dying on the cross and paying the penalty that was mine to pay. He did nothing wrong yet suffered. I, on the other hand, knew I made many mistakes, committed many sins daily, how could I complain when I made that comparison?

∞ Recognizing that struggles develop character—good or bad—that's our personal choice.

My Thoughts

_____

_____

_____

"We are troubled on every side, yet not distressed; we are perplexed, but not in despair; persecuted, but not forsaken; cast down, but not destroyed" (2 Corinthians 4:8–9).

PEARLS FOR OTHERS: "WHAT CAN I DO TO HELP?"

∞ Tell someone you know who is struggling that you love them and will be there to support them—and then follow through.

∞ Write a note of encouragement to someone you know who is struggling with a special-needs child or simply a difficult family situation (a quick handwritten note still holds more value than a quick e-mail! Everyone loves to get personal mail).

∞ If you see a mother struggling in a store/park with her children, why not offer to help her out rather than pass judgment—you never know if there's more behind the tantrum than an inconsistent mother and an undisciplined child.

∞ Actions go much further than advice; following through with your offer is what will truly impact another's life.

∞ If a mother you know suffers from a disease or is on bed rest with pregnancy, why not take a meal (even regularly) or organize a group to do so a few times a week; hire a cleaning service for her; plant some colorful flowers outside their home or bring pots pre-planted and drop them on the porch; offer to take her children for a day or commit to a regular scheduled time.

∞ The options are endless; this is just a list of a few areas to get your own thoughts running.

∞ Keep in mind that a mother in a challenging situation will likely appreciate your help in most any way, but be sure that the ideas you come up with are ones she is also comfortable with (for example, taking children out for the day would be nice, but if your plans will disrupt their nap time, then the mother may prefer not to accept your offer, as it would ultimately make her life more challenging when they return home). Make your offers with understanding and flexibility.

Ways I Commit to Help Someone I Know

_____

_____

_____

DISCOURAGING DIAGNOSIS

Determination:
Working to accomplish God's goals in God's
time regardless of the opposition. The abil-
ity to avoid words, actions, and attitudes which
could result in undesirable consequences [3]

Changes in Our Home

Discouragement definitely crept into the walls of our home—the walls in which we eventually hid ourselves by now. Though prior we had been a growing family out in our community and in the public eye through business and political avenues we attended with our children, meeting with figures like Vice President Dan Quayle, U.S. Senator Spencer Abraham, House Speaker Newt Gingrich, Congressmen J. D. Hayworth, U.S. Senator Lindsay Graham, governors, other elected officials, business people, and the like, we were now almost forced to remain at home. At least the boys and I were. Safe from the judgment of others' critical eyes and in a place that harm would not be inflicted upon outsiders due to the unpredictable bizarre behaviors we faced daily with our son, Richie. Wondering why just being a "boy" was so disturbing, I began to be convinced that we were failing as parents, something that you would rather not advertise in such a public way. So eventually, the children and I would have to remain home.

When Richie turned one, we had noticed that he stopped talking. Although his "talk" was just typical babbling baby talk, consisting of words like ba-ba, ma-ma and da-da, he was communicating and learning. Then right around twelve months, after his well check up he seemed to *lose* of all of his words. We had a busy life in business, politics, and a growing family coupled with my own health challenges, so I thought perhaps I was making something out of nothing. But along with his lack of talking, he no longer seemed to communicate his needs at all. He became easily frustrated and upset. Nothing we seemed to do would help. With no interest in self-help skills, he required much assistance in daily living. As I was pregnant with our fourth son, I noticed that many times Richie appeared to be deaf. He wouldn't respond at all to his name or any amount of calling unless I got right in his face, and even then he would sometimes look right through me.

Fixating himself on playing with a particular toy for hours while making a continuous motoring sound that would ring in our ears long after he went to sleep at night seemed never ending. After his brother's birth, the behaviors seemed to get worse. He seemed much more hyper and aggressive; if he wasn't fixated on something, he was likely disheartening or destroying something else. I finally went to the doctor only to be told this was typical *boy* behavior; since we had just brought home another new baby he was likely *acting out* or *withdrawing* for attention. All of the various behaviors I mentioned were excused for some reason of being a boy.

But, it just didn't seem *typical* to me. I had already brought home other new babies in which my older children transitioned well. We always included all the siblings with the arrival of a new baby. I had friends bringing new babies home and their toddlers weren't acting like Richie. But he was a *boy.* Perhaps we had a busier life than others I knew, and it was our schedule provoking these behavior challenges. He would talk one day, I tried to convince myself. I kept being told of great men of history who didn't talk and just one day started speaking in sentences, later to become some great historian whom I studied in years past. With that in mind I kept waiting and hoping for that day, focusing on the thought that perhaps he would grow up and be a "great" in history too.

As time went on, however, I realized that his aggressiveness and hyperactivity were such that I couldn't leave him alone in a room with any other child, as he would often hit, bite, shove, and throw toys, etc., to anyone around him for no apparent reason. Again, I sought out help and was continually told that he was just being a boy, and that I needed to be more consistent in discipline, that I shouldn't have had so many children, and on and on. If it was negative, I likely heard it. If it blamed me, I definitely heard it. I sought much prayer as I began to feel totally responsible and at the same time irresponsible, since I couldn't seem to be consistent enough to train this child to behave better. By now, his younger brother was also beginning to show signs of similar behaviors.

As I became pregnant again, I went back to the doctor determined that something was wrong and that I wouldn't leave until I got some answers. Since I could scream his name and he appeared deaf at times, I stood on the possibility that perhaps he was somewhat deaf and how could that be excused? So I was sent for speech and hearing testing at the children's hospital. No hearing issues, but he had little to no expressive language and the little speech he did have was back to beginning sounds—brief two-letter babbles but he still didn't communicate his needs. So, speech therapy came into play, and we also discovered that he suffered from verbal apraxia as well. His mouth and tongue had to be taught how to cooperate together to eat better and form words. We all learned how to teach him to communicate, even without language, by using a picture communication system and simple sign language program, which definitely helped in some ways with his frustration. I hadn't realized until that time that he never pointed to what he wanted; instead, he would just scream until we figured it out or he would take a person's hand and just lead them to the refrigerator or door or any area to which he desired something. Then the game of guessing came into play as we sought to figure out what he wanted or needed before he got so frustrated he would have a tantrum.

His behaviors became increasingly numbered. Below is a list I compiled for the doctor of the many behaviors he exhibited regularly at that time in his life:

∞ Rubbing (the arm of a family member), self-stimulating behavior
∞ Hyperactive
∞ Aggressive
∞ Resistant to change (in routine or furniture; anything)
∞ Inability to sit still at meals, constantly banging a glass
∞ Low threshold for frustration
∞ Crave and seeks the same foods
∞ High pain threshold
∞ Inability to feel compassion when hurting or offending others
∞ Unexpressive of normal responsive emotions
∞ Oversensitive at times
∞ Hypersensitivity to fabrics, tags, socks, etc.
∞ Major sensory issues to sounds, lights, stimuli
∞ Temper fits
∞ Unpredictable behavior

∞ Doesn't conform well to structured schedule (i.e.
∞ schooling)
∞ Excessively loud voice
∞ Violent at times
∞ Resistant/disobedient at times
∞ Hits fists together over and over again
∞ Hits head on floor or wall
∞ Takes silverware and bangs it on table or another
∞ dish repeatedly during meals
∞ Writes in scribbles, pushing very hard with pencil
∞ until breaking it at times during schooling
∞ Inability to concentrate on lessons taught or engage
∞ in conversation
∞ Overaggressive in defending siblings
∞ No fear of anything—runs off, climbs too high, runs
∞ in front of traffic, etc.
∞ Inability to obtain self-control when engaging in *any*
  activity. (i.e. begins rolling ball with another soon
  turns into throwing hard; gentle wrestle play can
  quickly turn into harsh, rough beating up; writing
  letters often turns into dark, hard scribbles, then rip-
  ping the page; etc.)
∞ Doesn't communicate needs
∞ Doesn't point
∞ Didn't speak until after speech therapy was begun
∞ Not developing self-help skills—has no interest

He also had a variety of physical symptoms that the
other children didn't seem to have, such as skin allergies
and stomach issues.

After the birth of our fifth child, Richie was three. A
dear friend of mine observed his behaviors one day and

suggested perhaps he had autism. Unfortunately the only vision/knowledge I had of autism was from two movies I had seen and neither portrayed the same behaviors I seemed to have with my son. She even gave me a book on the subject that, again, didn't seem to be exactly what I was dealing with. The doctor didn't think this was an issue so I didn't take her thoughts to heart as I should have. Later, however, I would reflect on her insight when doctors continued to not have an explanation for the many bazaar behaviors Richie had. I have consulted often with my dear friend Becca, who has helped guide me along some very deep waters.

Finally, one August when I began to homeschool the children, he was so disruptive and led the pack for his two younger siblings to follow his lead. And as children do, both younger brothers were promptly learning *how to act* by mimicking their older brother. Hence, they would imitate many of Richie's autistic behaviors. I was beyond belief at what a failure I was with boys. A turning point came during the first day of homeschooling my daughters that year, when my mother called mid-morning to see how it was going and I broke down in tears. I knew there was just no way I could do it any longer. She came and decided to take Richie home for the day, since the younger two boys were down for their morning naps. When they awoke and I began to correct their poor behaviors, which I had done daily with all three but to no avail, within about two hours I saw a total change in my home. I couldn't believe it. We actually ate a meal together and no one screamed, threw food, spun in their chair, banged glasses or threw a tantrum—they just ate! Our meal times with Richie likened the scene from the miracle worker where Annie Sullivan was trying to teach Helen Keller table manners, and it turned into quite a fight and flight scene. That was life for our family at *every* meal time. Hence, why we settled by that point to stay behind closed doors most of the time to avoid the judgment and embarrassment of being seen in public with such behaviors. I always feared we would end up on the front page of the local paper, since there was much talk in our small community about our family due to business and politics. I could just see those headlines reading, "The Chrysler Family; Leaders in the Community; Failures With Boys"! I feared for my father-in-law who was in Congress and loved his little grandson that in some way this kind of behavior or uncontrolled tantrum would become a negative plague for him. It was just too unpredictable to have Richie out during that season of life. So we opted to encapsulate ourselves in the safety of our home, trying desperately to figure out what was going wrong with our boys.

However, after Richie returned home that first evening from spending the day at my mother's and the level of stress climaxed once again, within minutes I realized it wasn't me or all the boys—something *was* wrong with our oldest son. But what? The remainder of that week my mother took Richie home with her each day after breakfast and he returned after dinner. This was the turning point discovery for our family, and I will be ever grateful for my mother's insight and commitment in taking him home that week. Her health didn't allow her to continue this schedule permanently. And I never wanted to ask for and receive such continuous help with the basics, as I felt I should be able to handle my children myself. After all, others did. And I was the one who desired all these children, so I should be able to take care of them. Right? All I needed to do was find out what was wrong with my oldest son and *fix it,* so then we could be a less-stressed family once again.

What a turn around that week without Richie brought. Laughter, peace, and joy! We played games, went to the park, out to lunch, grocery shopping, and that was still with four young children, but it was just like all my friends did! We were a normal family doing typical family activities together. Life was fun once more—I could enjoy being a mother and not just feeling like some kind of exhausted, overworked surveillance officer on duty 24/7. What relief in one respect. I now knew it wasn't something *I* was doing terribly wrong with all my boys. But what could it be? I had certainly applied all those helpful child training books. So off to the doctor we went. I now had proof that something indeed was wrong with my oldest son. It had become more than just his speech and ability to communicate. I couldn't wait to get some answers and some help.

The initial doctor's trip led us on a trail of various doctor appointments; from psychologist to psychiatrist to neurologist we went. The details of which really don't matter at this point. But suffice it to say that he was given many different combinations of diagnoses, depending on the doctor we saw. The list consisted of a combination of the following: ADD, ADHD, OCD, conduct disorder, high functioning autism, autism, ASD, Asperger's, bipolar disorder, and PDD NOS—at this point I really didn't know what to think or believe. Either he was certainly complex, or diagnosing his symptoms was not going to be easy. It seemed wherever we went they would derive one to three different diagnoses for him. Yet, the prognosis was always grim. No hope, no treatment, no future.

Since I had spent time studying in the medical library in college I assumed there must be more information I could find, so I set out to research and decipher what was going on. I had to know which of these disorders he *really* had. No one knew my son better than I did. During this time Richie did see a neurologist and discovered he had been having mild seizures, likely in his sleep. After much study, research, and additional testing, it was conclusive that Richie had autism. I give thanks to Dr. Bernie Rimland and Dr. Sidney Baker for their efforts co-founding the "Defeat Autism Now!" organization, which was our final resting place to sort out the various diagnoses that Richie had been given and conclude the diagnosis of autism. That was a bittersweet discovery. Of course, I was glad that there wasn't something terribly wrong with all three boys, but at the same time the prognosis was grim to say the least. There was no medication to help, no specific treatment, some forms of therapy might help a little, but we were told that as bad as Richie was by then, he was five, the future was quite hopeless.

One particular doctor tried to convince us more than once the best treatment plan would be to institutionalize him. I'll never forget his words, "You can't let one bad apple ruin the whole batch. You have four other children and your marriage to consider." This doctor also had a son with autism who was in an institution. He was the first one that brought the devastating reality to our faces. Although I was living with Richie 24/7 and certainly realized the challenges I faced moment by moment living behind closed doors with his unusual behaviors, and I could see the effects clearly on the rest of the family, I couldn't imagine putting him in some institution; nor could the rest of our family. There were moments of tenderness, when he would rub my arm to fall asleep every night, when tears would stream down my face as I thought of him alone in some institution—no mother there for him to count on, *no* hope for a future. I just couldn't accept that fate for him. I didn't believe that God would give me a child, allow him to be damaged and develop autism, yet not give me what I needed to help him. I just knew there had to be another way and that became my focus—keeping my son out of an institution. How grateful I am this day that I didn't give up.

It was at this time that my mother heard of a special featuring a young man with autism airing on Oprah. So she watched the special interview of a man, Thomas McKean, who had autism and experienced time in an institution. He had written a book about his experiences, *Soon Will Come the Light,* so she ordered it for me since she knew of our struggles praying about putting Richie in an institution. After quickly reading through his book, especially the sections about institution life, through tears of conviction I vowed I would do what it took to prevent my son from ever having to be put in an institution himself. I am grateful to Thomas McKean for writing his book; it made a huge impact in our family's life.

But being told the statistics of Richie not getting better coupled with the statistics of the divorce rate in families with autism, along with having four other children to raise, it was hard to conceive what I was being told or how it would work out. It was hard to imagine there was any other way. My dreams, at this point, were completely shattered. Our once-happy family singing at local Right to Life and campaign events, walking in parades, myself speaking to women's groups on marriage and children— shattered. All of it, over.

As my husband and I cried together, I prayed and prayed that there must be some other way. What? I had no idea. I had to admit the effects of his behavior were already deeply affecting our marriage and clearly affecting the other children. Not to mention living any kind of *normal* lifestyle. The stress and strain daily was insurmountable. What did I have to stand on to refute that doctor's advice not instituting my son? But a cold, isolated institution? Far away from the family who loved him? Why? Because something had damaged him and caused this dreaded disorder to overtake his body. But an institution? There had to be another way.

I recall seeking many friends and asking for prayer. I quickly committed myself to learning all I could about autism and what could be done. Were the doctors we saw all right? Was there really no hope? It had to have been all the prayers that gave me the determination to press on and seek another answer. It wasn't easy. With a nursing baby and four other children, my studies couldn't even *begin* until about 11:30 at night after the baby went to bed. And I would study until around two a.m. nightly until I just couldn't stay awake any longer. Then rising early to begin my day writing in my prayer journal, seeking God's Word for wisdom and direction, I would try to trust Him with this unforeseen future.

Although it wasn't easy and our life was in constant turmoil then, I am grateful that I didn't give up or give in to what I was being advised with my son. My heart ached too much to think of locking my son away, having strangers take care of him. Yet, I could also totally understand why that doctor did so himself. Life was hard! No, it was *worse* than hard. It was unbearable at times. His behaviors were like being in constant unpredictable torment with four other innocent bystanders. I had to constantly consciously remind myself that *he* didn't *want* to act this way and *he needed my help.* I began to rest on a few particular verses of the Bible to get me through, repeating them over and over again throughout the days, months, and years that followed: Proverbs 3:5–6 "Trust in the Lord with all thine heart and lean not unto thine own understanding. In all thy ways acknowledge Him and He shall direct thy paths." And Romans 8:28: "And we know that all things work together for good to them that love God; to them who are called according to his purpose." I would usually write one verse a day, one that stuck out to me in that morning's reading, [on a 3x5 card,] and set it before me wherever I was. If I had not done that I truly don't know if I would have made it through all I did. Resting on God's strength was my greatest hope. By this time I felt quite alone in my life behind closed doors with my five children, my husband gone to the business and then off to evening political meetings. It was a very lonely, isolated feeling.

Developing flexibility, our days consisted of rising by five a.m. to begin schooling the girls before Richie and the babies woke up. Our "school day" was an early one but it worked. Flexibility and creativity were a must. We got all the major items accomplished during our early morning hours prior to anyone else rising. Then, once the boys all awoke, we would begin our day of trying to learn and control this invader seeking to destroy our family called autism. Try hard as I would, Richie's breakdowns would occur for any reason at all up to ten times a day, lasting anywhere from ten to sixty minutes while I would have to hug him tight to prevent him from escaping and hurting himself or others. I recall one day the children were in the family room and as I began making lunch, I went to them three times explaining they needed to prepare to stop soon, as lunch was almost ready. When I went once more to tell the children to come for lunch, Richie began to scream, trying to grab his siblings to keep everyone how they had been. No changes could take place without him breaking down. Whether it was that, having to go somewhere in the car, moving the furniture, wearing a different shirt, nothing could change. Nothing.

When a change did occur and a breakdown resulted, our *little hide-and-seek routine* would quickly take place. Each daughter was assigned a younger brother to whisk up and take to the bedroom. They were to go quickly and lock the door in case I couldn't get to Richie in time to prevent him from hurting someone. I would then have to hold him with all my might, keeping him from banging his head, hurting himself in some way, or running off to hurt someone else. I later learned this was the exact way the therapists would teach us to handle his breakdowns. During these meltdowns I was head-butted, scratched, kicked, bruised, had my hair pulled out—it wasn't easy, but it was our life with autism. He would finally go limp in my arms and be fine to lie down or he would actually fall into a deep sleep as I hugged him through tears, wondering why this was happening to him. I began to wonder how I was going to manage as he grew older and stronger. I was already beginning to have a hard time holding him at age four. I knew I had to study harder and find a better way to help him.

Discretion was important to me so that the difficult breakdown behaviors wouldn't affect the other children negatively. For the girls I made this a game and a special time that they got to spend with their baby brothers and praised them for helping so much. They got to *plan* the fun *hide-and-seek* time by reading, telling stories, or playing with blocks with their little brothers. This was just the routine we had to have to survive, and thankfully, they were both mature and responsible to play as asked. They actually thought it a fun time with their baby brothers while they played mommy as little girls love to do. And they always knew they could call me if needed. Keeping everyone safe and in as healthy an environment as possible with an autistic sibling was my goal. This was important to me since those words of the doctor saying autism could "ruin the whole batch" of our children were fresh in my mind. I didn't want to put Richie in an institution, yet I wanted to protect our other children from being a "soiled batch." I confess, though, that I was growing more and more weary, wondering how much longer we could continue life in this way. It was a time where you just do what you have to and use it to motivate you to search out answers. This life definitely motivated me to continue researching nightly and not give up. Something had to change. But there seemed to be no other option.

So, I just kept praying, having faith and determination, doing what I had to do to survive each day.

The verses that I ingrained in my mind each night to get to sleep were:

"Therefore do not worry about tomorrow, for tomorrow will worry about itself. Each day has enough trouble of its own" (Matthew 6:34, NIV).

"And he said unto me, my grace is sufficient for thee: for my strength is made perfect in weakness. Most gladly therefore will I rather glory in my infirmities, that the power of Christ may rest upon me" (2 Corinthians 12:9).

REFLECTIONS FOR RECOVERY

∞ Do you have the determination to do what you need to, regardless of how hopeless it seems? If you don't think so, then reach deeper inside and realize there is a hidden bounty of strength in each of us, just waiting to be tapped into.

∞ Go to the Lord for all of your strength, search out scriptures that reflect our need to rely on Him when situations seem hopeless. He promises, "My grace is sufficient for thee: for my strength is made perfect in weakness" (2 Corinthians 12:9a).

∞ Write on a 3x5 card these verses and try to commit some to memory; during those exasperating times they will give you strength to keep going. Stick them on the walls so they are ever before you.

∞ Is your home engulfed with a challenge? If so, have you made it as fun as possible for your other children? Do they know how special and helpful they are? If not, ask them how they are feeling and set out to praise them daily. Communication is critical.

∞ If you are in a situation that is more than you can handle, seek help. Don't allow yourself to get frustrated and lose your temper and integrity—seek help from someone who will listen and cares for you. Share this book and highlight what you most need help with or use it to trigger those things that would most help in your life and then create your own list.

My Own Thoughts

_____

_____

_____

Pearls for Others: "What can I do to help?"

∞ If you know of someone who is struggling, offer to help out.
∞ Take the other children out on a regular basis
∞ Take the special-needs child out on a regular basis
∞ Help with housework or other areas that might be slipping
∞ Help that person research for treatment options— there's many things that can be done
∞ Encourage those parents to keep pushing forward— nothing good is ever easy and usually if it is easy, it won't last long
∞ Help them not to give up or give in
∞ Don't judge, just help!

Ways I Commit to Help Someone I Know

_____

_____

_____

DIET DECISIONS

Diligence:
Visualizing each task as a special assignment from
the Lord and using all my energies to accomplish it[4]

Prior to all the doctor treatments and therapies we would learn were critical to Richie's recovery, I first learned of some dietary changes that alone brought some children to recovery. The more I studied on diets the more hope I had for our son's recovery. Yet, I would soon realize that for most, my son included, recovering from autism is like a puzzle, and it takes many, many pieces before you have a beautiful picture of recovery to look at. And unlike most puzzles with the completed picture to guide you— the puzzle of autism comes blank for each child. There are many pieces to choose from. Some fit into place in a child's life and begin to bring the picture into clearer focus, while others are placed on the sidelines and you're not quite sure how they contribute to the finished framework. Sometimes they are simply the *extras* that are just the background and sidelines, but without trying them in the center picture you simply wouldn't know where they fit. So, I looked at each intervention we tried as a viable piece to complete our puzzle of autism.

I mentioned earlier I initially decided that although this new diet seemed difficult, no gluten (the wheat protein, which is hidden in many foods) and no casein (the dairy protein also hidden in many foods), I needed to try it. It was a starting block for us. Cutting out casein, the dairy protein, was our first attempt. The results amazed us! Within three days Richie's severe breakdowns with the aggression began to lessen! We began to see a new glimmer of light shine through. I quickly fixated on the fact that if I learned how to cut out gluten also, my son would be cured like the other children I read about! How excited we all were. But soon we found that although the gluten-free diet did produce some additional improvements that were significant enough not to stop this special diet, we were nowhere near *cured*.

This new diet lent itself to increased stress in shopping, cooking, and feeding my family of seven. From all the changes I had made years prior due to treating lupus naturally, I really thought we were eating quite healthy. We ate mostly organic foods, ground our own wheat berries, and made our own homemade delicious bread daily. Healthy as it seemed, all those grains had to go. Often homemade cheese bread was a staple for our family. The cheese and other dairy products were not as hard to give up, but the bread—that was everyone's favorite! Having five children, homemade whole grain bread seemed a very healthy way to provide whole grain breakfasts, lunches, and snacks. Now I realized my *healthy whole grains* were causing havoc for my son's brain!

Cutting out all these items, we learned, had to be done for the entire family since Richie seemed to be able to locate gluten in our home no matter where we might hide it. We had to rid our home completely of all gluten and casein, realizing that if he consumed even a bite of something off this diet there would be some visible and often major autistic behaviors crop back up.

As I researched and we did further testing, we learned that Richie ended up having some forty-five additional food allergies to all the other foods he ate. He already had many issues with food tastes and textures and now we were about to take all the fruits, vegetables, meats, and grains away that I knew he would eat and I knew how to prepare. But life had to change. We learned that you can get flour from beans, eat ostrich and buffalo meat, and create meals with those funny-looking fruits and vegetables that I never thought anyone purchased, let alone could pronounce the name of and prepare for edible consumption! This was quite a learning experience to say the least.

Thus, I embarked on yet another adventure in life. My happily-ever-after dream family continued to take me to new heights and depths. My focus was not to fall off or drown in the process. But those long past days of colic looked easy compared to where I was now. Perhaps that was God's way to help gradually build my endurance to weather this storm before me. Through consistence and diligence we persevered. Richie's behaviors where improving to a degree that made my other children vow to stay on our difficult diet for the moments of peaceful playtime we could experience intermittently throughout the day. He was far from recovered, but that flicker of occasional light gave me renewed drive to press on. A variety of autistic behaviors were still an issue, and I constantly wondered if I was feeding him something wrong where there was hidden gluten or casein in a food that hindered him from getting completely better. Thus the search for a doctor and additional treatment continued.

Everyone seemed to actually feel better on this new approach to eating. However, we did soon realize that drive-through restaurants were out of the question, and those quick trips for bagels or other pre-made meals disappeared. This added new challenges for me. Having Lupus and raising five young children, coupled with autism, while in the midst of a political campaign, planning ahead for meals and cooking the right foods all the time was quite a chore. I am much more delighted in cooking what sounds good on a given day and enjoying the spontaneity of life. Getting caught up in a hike through the fields and woods with my children returning home to simply whipping up a box of macaroni and cheese with breaded chicken breasts on a bun with a vegetable (I knew the name of) was always nice to do. Not now. That was no longer an option. Even all those organic boxes of quick foods that didn't have all the bad preservatives, additives, and colors in them were no longer an option for us. At that time there didn't seem to be anything quick and easy to cook from packaged foods that would be *allowed* on Richie's diet. I am grateful to the many companies giving more options of quick GFCF (gluten free casein free) foods now available. However, the convenience of these pre-made foods comes with a much larger price tag so unless a family has endless funds this, often is not an option. Often baking foods from scratch is still the only choice.

The average homemade gluten-free recipe consisted of about fifteen ingredients. Cooking from scratch, especially that scratchy, was just not something I had time to do much of. Aside from our homemade bread and perhaps muffins, I did not search out to do that much lengthy kind of baking. I was just too busy with five young children and political life. Not to mention the times I did take baking GFCF cookies or bread only to have it end in a pile of crumbs and taste like cardboard, which seemed such a waste of time and money, neither of which I could afford to waste. In addition to the long list of ingredients, there were items I had never even heard of. Things that weren't available in the local grocery or health food store and sometimes were only available from limited resources online that could take hours to find and cost considerable amounts of money. So talk about a major change in planning for me. This was one of my biggest personal challenges in Richie's recovery process.

My mother learned how to prepare many of the special foods that we now needed for our family. She would often concentrate on making batches of *special treats* like cookies or brownies (without having gluten, casein, eggs, sugar, or some other forbidden ingredient) that we could keep frozen for special family gatherings so Richie would have a special dessert he could eat. I was so grateful for her help in these areas. But I was still struggling with having babies, Richie's behavior challenges, homeschooling, maintaining our outside ministry and political commitments, while maintaining the daily preparation of foods.

I finally relinquished control of my kitchen and humbled myself, admitting that I just couldn't keep up with these additional demands on my schedule and accepted a generous offer for a friend's daughter, Carrie Beeman, to come a few days a week to help me out. She was the oldest daughter of eight children and came with many skills I hadn't truly developed in the area of organizing my kitchen and meals for so many. She took my resources home, studied them, and came back ready to tackle the job. Quickly learning his needs, she created many ready-made *mixes* for us to use that consisted of just those items Richie could tolerate. What a tremendous help she was. She also baked many items for us that we froze and then I could pull out during those busy times. She became a valuable resource to our family during a precious time of personal growth for me.

One of the greatest things I have learned in life is that if I am humble and do not allow pride to enter into even my thoughts, then I can learn something from practically anyone. "Better it is to be of a humble spirit with the lowly, than to divide the spoil with the proud" (Proverbs 16:19). Each of us has a unique gift and different qualities. I have gleaned so much from so many people throughout our course of recovering Richie, the list would seem exhaustive to write. Many times in my past I would have never wanted to admit that someone else had a better way of doing something, if I had already taken time to figure something out. But often, I would reflect on their idea and if I hadn't given myself over to pride, I would recognize the value in it. Now I try to always remember that I don't have to defend my methods or ideas; instead I listen to and consider what others have to say. Then I can take the information and discern what to do. There is so much growth we can experience when we keep a humble attitude. God seems to continue to give me opportunities to humble myself. Often our lives can be saved from so much turmoil if we listen more than we talk.

I have since sought to teach my daughters how to cook all these foods, and for the past few years my oldest daughter, Chloe, has done all of our GFCF cooking, continuing where our young friend left off. Chloe began on her own when she was about twelve learning how to make a recipe with fifteen ingredients work. She even wrote a little GFCF cookbook *From Kids for Kids!* (See appendix for cookbook.) Developing a love for cooking now, at fifteen she does meal planning, grocery list preparation, and most all of our family's cooking. She has enjoyed the task of taking some of our favorite recipes and converting them into GFCF meals that the whole family can enjoy. I am hardly in the kitchen anymore, and I am so grateful for her and her sister, Heather, who is following in her footsteps at twelve! This is part of the reason I did have time to write this book! I owe much to my two daughters.

As a matter of fact, during the writing process of this book I had need for a quiet place to set up and write. One day I returned from some errands to find that my daughters had decided to surprise me. My recently turned thirteen-year-old and her fifteen-year-old sister moved all their things together into one bedroom to share. They then set up a writing room for me in the other. It came complete with everything I needed and then some. What a huge surprise and blessing to experience such a gift from my teenage daughters who were willing to give up their space to make this book a reality. I'm so grateful for all that we've endured as a family since I feel these life experiences have produced shiny red apples in our children over those *bad apples* I was warned of by keeping our son at home. I certainly don't want to imply we are a perfect family with perfect children, but I believe if we follow our heart how the Lord leads, He will bless. I'm grateful I did that with keeping Richie home.

"Train up a child in the way he should go: and when he is old he will not depart from it" (Proverbs 22:6).

REFLECTIONS FOR RECOVERY

∞ Are you willing to make sacrifices in your lifestyle and refrigerator for a better life and future for your family, if that's what it takes?

∞ If your child was *deathly* allergic to peanuts, would you keep them out of the house and request that others do the same? If so, then realize that you can do what needs to be done for your child on any restrictive diet, just put it in perspective whatever it might be. (For some it is temporary as well.) Remember: short-term sacrifice for long-term gain.

∞ Are you willing to ask/accept help in your kitchen? In your home? With any area that simply has you overwhelmed? Humble yourself and experience the blessing!

My Own Thoughts

_____

_____

_____

PEARLS FOR OTHERS: "WHAT CAN I DO TO HELP?"

∞ Get educated on a child's special dietary needs and offer to go shopping to read all the labels and find the foods necessary.

∞ Offer to watch children so the parents can go shopping for special foods or other items needed.

∞ Research online for resources to purchase foods.

∞ Give a gift card for online or health food stores that carry the necessary foods a child needs since they can be very expensive.

∞ Offer to bake and freeze items for future use (especially useful are special treats like brownies, cupcakes, etc. so they will be on hand when a special event arises like a birthday party).

∞ Research recipes and create "mixes" for the family to quickly use for baking.

Ways I Commit to Help Someone I Know

_____

_____

_____

DOCTORS AND THERAPIES

Decisiveness:
The ability to recognize key fac-
tors and finalize difficult decisions[5]

After embarking upon much research I began to learn that there were a few doctors that were treating and, it seemed, making progress with children on the autism spectrum. I began to intently research all I could. Initially I found a doctor about two hours from our home that specialized in treating autism through a biomedical approach (where and why symptoms originated from). This was what I had been reading about on the DAN! Web site, and he was a doctor who had attended their training conference. I was elated to find someone so close to my home and taking new patients. With everything I had researched I had no idea where I would start or what I would do, but I recognized that a biomedical approach to treatment was the only route that gave me hope for success. I made an appointment and anticipated the day that I would get some help, hope, and direction. How grateful I was to locate a doctor close enough to drive to that specialized in children with autism.

I'll never forget the day of that appointment. I made the difficult two-hour journey alone with all five children. Upon our arrival to the office I noticed American flags hanging all around the exterior and interior of the office. But with the recent terrorist attack on September 11, just weeks prior to my appointment, flags hanging were a pretty common sight, so reflecting on what our country was facing I had a moment to compare my own war I was waging against autism. We had over an hour wait. When I was finally called back it seemed quite chaotic and then a different doctor came in to see us. I asked about the doctor we were to see who specialized in autism; she practically broke down telling me that he was a reserve officer and was going off to war later that very day due to the terrorist attack. How grateful I was to know he was a man willing to keep us all safe, yet how defeated I felt as my hope for immediate help with my son deflate. The office was in a flurry, trying to figure out how they were going handle his patients since he alone was the one working with all these autistic children. Although I didn't lose a loved one from that terrible day, 9–11, I felt I had lost hope for reaching my son, for unlocking him out of the prison of autism. It was amazing to me how this terrorist attack had ultimately succeeded in destroying even more lives than just those lost on that dreaded day. Prior to that day in September I had also been asked by Congressman Dan Burton to testify before Congress regarding autism and the epidemic increase it was having. But that testimony got put on a back burner indefinitely due to the terrorist attacks.

The doctor's office did some testing, most of which I requested based on what I had learned from my reading and research. But two weeks later when I returned for the results I saw yet another doctor, as they were still trying to cope with the loss of their specialist in treating autistic children. As we went through the test results and I asked what to do now and questioned some of the treatments that I had studied, I recall this doctor looking at me and apologizing but explaining that none of the other doctors normally saw and treated these autistic children. This specialist in autism, now far around the world defending our country, was involved in doing all the research and documentation, so he alone had been seeing and treating all the children with autism. It would take them some time before they could study all his research and determine the best modes of treatment for a new patient. But

I had already learned that time was of the essence. I had already lost three or more years not realizing what was attacking my son's abilities, and now how much longer could we wait? How much more could my family endure with autism?

I left there with many test results but no treatment plan. Feeling devastated didn't explain my true emotions. By this time the rollercoaster of emotions was more than nauseating. I already knew there were no other doctors closer than a few states away. When I did research those doctors, not one of them was taking new patients. It seemed too far to drive back to this clinic as the only doctor I thought could treat us was now gone. There were so few truly *treating* children with autism at that time and in a way that was producing positive results, so for those who did, they were sought after quickly.

Back to intense prayer and studying. "Every purpose is established by counsel: and with good advice maketh war" (Proverbs 22:18). I realized I really was making war against autism. I gathered everything I could from the medical library and every resource I could get online. I interpreted test results, consulted with compounding pharmacists and biologists, documented everything, figured out what I needed done next, and proceeded to see my pediatrician. I put before her all the information I had gathered to document the additional tests and treatments I wanted to pursue for my son. The stack was many inches thick, organized in a binder to make her job of reading my research as easy as possible. I explained my dilemma with finding a specialized doctor and my desire to get my son treated with biomedical interventions. So she agreed to study what I presented to her and help me

treat my son. I am so grateful to this day for her willingness to work with us and get us started on our road to
recovery. I could have been angry and bitter that she had
not diagnosed him during the three earlier years I went
back with concerns. But that would not have accomplished anything for any of us.

Together, we set out to learn and treat his autism the
best we knew how. She ordered additional testing that I
requested until I found everything I needed to know at
that point where his body wasn't functioning properly.
But exactly how to treat and fix it was another dilemma.
Around that time I was able to attend a DAN! (Defeat
Autism Now) conference in San Diego, California, where
doctors from around the world gathered to share their
insights and results in treating children with autism.
Here, I was able to talk with and listen to the many doctors that were having positive results treating patients
with autism. I gathered all the information I could and
put our name on one to three-year waiting lists for the
physicians that had a list and would accept him due to
his age.

I returned home and soon suffered acute appendicitis
attack. I had to go to the hospital emergency, but it was
so crowded I ended up waiting hours until I could have
surgery. The severe pain subsided a bit so while waiting, I was able to tackle all the reading material from the
conference. As God does things, He worked that time
for good for me to study. I was able to read throughout
the entire DAN Protocol book and discover what to do
with all those test results and how to begin treating my
son. Using every moment to its maximum was a concept
I gleaned from the Scriptures, especially Ephesians 5:16,

"Redeeming the time because the days are evil." Thus, I almost always carry a bag or briefcase with reading or research material…just in case I get a few minutes somewhere. Little did I think I would get so much reading and studying done in the ER awaiting surgery! Though I never expected to have that kind of wait before surgery, I was grateful I had brought my bag with all my research in it for autism. It was funny, as the doctors came repeatedly apologizing for the delay, I reassured them that I was grateful, as I never could have had that much study time at home with my five young children. Not to mention that I'm not fond of having surgery and would rather endure pain and put it off! I really believe they may have put other patients in front of me because I was so content to wait. Once they learned what I was studying, one nurse asked me to share my insights with her, as she also knew someone recently diagnosed with autism. I completed the entire DAN protocol book for treatment and was able to analyze my son's tests, and after consulting with biologist William Shaw and my pediatrician, we set out where to begin.

With the help of my pediatrician, we began a series of biological treatments. Richie was making improvements. He had initially responded very well to a gluten-free and casein-free diet and as a result, his consistently major breakdown bouts dissipated. He became less aggressive and hyper. As we continued down the road to recovery, we discovered that he had over fifty different additional food allergies. Immunolabs out of Ft. Lauderdale has been one of our starting and maintaining places. So those were also eliminated. Chelation therapy removed the toxic heavy metals from his body and then we addressed the yeast build up of toxins.

We were in the midst of doing a variety of these treatments when it became obvious that I was surpassing all the knowledge I had gathered and now my pediatrician and I needed expert help in this biomedical approach to his recovery. I felt I just couldn't stop in the midst of all we had going, and she felt she could no longer proceed with limited knowledge. Richie was showing signs of improvement and was losing many of his symptoms, yet was still clearly with autistic behaviors. I couldn't go on at that point without expert help. There were too many variables, more testing needed, balancing each of the overlapping treatments I was doing. I became extremely anxious that I was at a point of no return with nowhere to go for direction. But as I prayed, God's Word in Philippians 4:6–7 became my focal point, "Be anxious for nothing, but in everything by prayer and supplication, with thanksgiving, let your requests be made known to God; and the peace of God which surpasses all understanding will guard your hearts and minds through Christ Jesus" (NKJV).

So after much prayer, I contacted all the doctors whose waiting lists I was on with no hope of getting in any time in the near future. Out of desperation and determination, I then contacted another doctor leading the course for treating autism. The one who had authored the book I had been treating out of—the DAN! Protocol for treatment. I had heard him speak at the conference and just knew he could help me. He also was not taking new patients, but by the grace of God, Dr. Sidney Baker agreed to see us. He was one of the leading doctors at these conferences as the co-founder and Medical Director of Defeat Autism Now! and co-author of the treatment protocol book I was referencing. I was filled with gratitude and praise to God, yet we were about to embark on new challenges of aggressive biomedical intervention to defeat my son's autism. We went from basically self-teaching ourselves on the bunny hill to hopping on the chair lift and rising to the top of a very tall mountain. I wouldn't realize how high I was until I got off the chair lift. It was then I would recognize the only hope down to recovery was much steeper than I had ever imagined. How glad I was to have a caring, compassionate, encouraging leader and coach by my side when I arrived. Without Dr. Baker, I'm not sure I could have done all I needed to with Richie, who was considered a bit old to begin treatment for hope of recovery. Richie's age did not stop Dr. Baker, which gave me inspired hope. There were even some doctors who had refused to take our name on their waiting lists because Richie was too old to treat with any hope of success. But Dr. Baker was different. He is the type of doctor who doesn't just tell you "this is what you need to do"; he then gives you the gentle, loving push and creative ideas to implement treatment and get started down the slope. I'm so grateful to Dr. Baker and his wonderful staff for the love and dedication they all commit to their patients.

While we were grateful beyond belief, a whole new entity awaited us. Traveling across the nation to the East Coast became our new *road to recovery* as we sought expert advice and treatment from Dr. Baker. Those trips are a story in itself! Traveling with an autistic child and his four siblings with all the above mentioned behaviors on a twelve-plus-hour road trip was always full of excitement and adventure. But thanks to Dr. Baker's wisdom, encouragement, and direction, Richie began making major strides.

Not only was Richie making strides, but it was at his first appointment with Dr. Baker that he looked at me and my history as Richie's mother with Lupus and mentioned a few things I could do for myself. Shortly after returning home to Michigan, I began seeing Dr. Tammy Born who treated my Lupus in a similar manner that we approached Richie's autism. The good news was that for the first time I began to be completely symptom free, not just symptom manageable. But the greater news is that during the final stages of writing this manuscript I was tested and my Lupus blood tests came back negative! This was the first time ever since 1992, after experiencing almost all the criteria for a Lupus diagnosis, that I tested negative. So I, too, have recovered from Lupus as a result of treating Richie for autism. Sometimes blessings are in disguise.

As we had been having these additional lab tests done to figure out what was in and out of balance in Richie's system creating symptoms with autism that were out of control, the bills began to filter in. One after another. $100 here, $350 there, most all expenses were rarely covered by insurance. Soon the monies were going out faster than they were coming in. Between doctor bills, travel expenses, continual lab tests, treatments, and soon-to-be therapies, not to mention the new increased grocery expense of gluten-free and casein-free foods, the bills increased at an amazing rate. We soon learned that although doctors were learning and treating autism and gaining positive results (as we were beginning to experience), insurance companies were declining coverage for tests or treatments for autism. But we were committed at this point. The more I learned, the greater became our hope for a promised future for our son—and ultimately our family.

Recognizing the various therapies that could help our son was our next adventure. There was speech therapy, which we were already involved in; occupational therapy; physical therapy; ABA therapy; sensory integration therapy; auditory integration therapy; light therapy; vision therapy; and the list goes on. Life was beginning to see glimpses of hope, and I didn't want to miss that *key puzzle piece* that would give us a *cure* to his autism. The more I studied, the more I heard promises that this therapy or that treatment brought another child to complete recovery. Of course, when hearing such things it's easy to cast all your effort into one particular arena, hoping that one treatment or therapy would be the *magic pill* to recovery. I would eventually learn that it was a combination of everything we tried that brought final victory and recovery for our son. But overall—we had to be committed for the long haul. Recovery is a process; achievement is a perspective.

Thankfully, Rick had been quite a good saver and investor and I was used to living frugally to help increase our savings from the very beginning, so we had funds accumulated to access for all these escalating costs. Rick worked very hard, but by that time due to this affliction upon our family, autism had not only been stealing our son away, it left its ugly mark on our finances and Rick's future goals career-wise.

For that moment, my focus was determining which treatments to do, how much to do, how to make it all work with our scheduling, and who to use to implement it. We couldn't worry about cost if it meant recovery. We had come so far. We couldn't stop now. We couldn't hold back on what might be that *final piece* to Richie's Recovery Puzzle. Our days were filled with trips to a lab, doctor, and therapists, or seeking out resources to purchase the costly new foods and supplements.

We schooled early and then set out on our road to recovery. It was sometimes slippery, sleeting, and difficult to stay the course; other times it was filled with ruts and muddy water. I recall having one therapist come out for a consultation for ABA in-home therapy. We were very new at ABA therapy and didn't really understand all the modalities. She spent a couple of hours with us, watching our son's behavior and stepping outside for about four cigarettes as she appeared quite anxious. She observed his inability to cooperate, his aggressiveness, lack of focus, and other lack of social and self-help skills. She then concluded that he might need tranquilizing medication since he was getting bigger and stronger and was still so aggressive and hard to handle while trying to get him to comply. Showing us how she could get him to cooperate by giving him candy to do a simple task, she handed over her bill for that consultation alone—$750 on site!

Desperate parents of a child with autism must be discerning when it comes to hiring therapists, doctors, and any help for that matter. Unfortunately, as with everything in our society, parents must use wisdom. "A wise man will hear, and will increase learning; and a man of understanding shall attain unto wise counsels" (Proverbs

1:5). Gratefully, if it weren't for our speech therapist, Anne Marie Balzer, we found through the local school system who had studied much in working with autistic children and some of our other OT, PT, and ABA therapists, we never would have achieved the results we did with our son. There are many great therapists out there, so parents just have to be selective, communicate their needs, and be willing to politely ask for another therapist if the personalities and goals don't mesh.

Including Siblings for Recovery

Since I was homeschooling and we did our lessons prior to all of our appointments, I would almost always bring at least one of Richie's siblings (if not all of them) along with us to his therapy appointments. Although, at times I had to explain my thoughts and ask to have them included in his therapy, this proved to be another turning point in his progress. Since his siblings were the ones he played with most of the time, they all learned how to draw out communication with him through speech therapy, implement OT techniques when he got too hyper, included fun PT therapies with their play, and even used ABA techniques with his behavior. Back at home I would schedule out our play time, and the older children would have scheduled times to *play* with him. During this time as I observed, the girls would automatically use the same terminology and methods that were being modeled to them during Richie's therapy appointments.

On each updated evaluation, Richie was making greater and faster strides than expected across the board. It was at that point when most all of our therapists encouraged us to continue bringing the other children, one at a time, to his appointments. I also included bringing anyone else who would spend much time with him, my parents, a friend, etc. I would rotate who would join us so that each person had adequate exposure to the different therapies. Although not everyone was able to join us, those that could help increased his progress.

What a difference it began to make. Most everyone was on the same page, using the same terms consistently bringing out his communication, handling his meltdowns in the same way. This consistency was a huge factor in bringing Richie along so quickly. Since we had not even begun much of his intervention, aside from a little speech therapy, until he was between five or six years old, we felt he was getting a late start for the hope of recovery. Through all my studies I discovered that early diagnosis and interventions applied by two to three years old had the best success. I continually felt cheated at times as we seemed to race against the clock, trying to fit it all in to make the progress he needed before it was *too late.*

But thinking of what could have been or what should have been was something I would learn I had no time to ponder. The focus was the here and now. Isaiah 43:18 says, "Remember ye not the former things, neither consider the things of old. Behold, I will do a new thing; now it shall spring forth, shall ye not know it. I will make a way in the wilderness and rivers in the desert." It felt like I was often walking through the desert much of the time. I was tired but I tried hard to implement what I had learned. My days were well documented with schedules for everything, tracking of all the medication/ supplements Richie needed. And I *had* been a person who enjoyed the spontaneity of life without strict routines and schedules. This completely new structured way of life was certainly not an easy change for me. Below is a chart that shows one season of Richie's protocol and how I tracked it. Dr. Baker made it so much easier to navigate through the priorities in Richie's biomedical treatments and so we continued to do all we could.

Time	Name	Stored	Amount	How Given
	BEFORE WAKING			
Before waking	TTFD / Glutithione Cream	Closet Shelf	.5 cc each	Use glove put TTFD on bottom of foot, Glut. On forearm
	BEFORE BREAKFAST			
Early Morning Before Breakfast	Nystatin	Refrigerator	1 teaspoon	Take without food straight off teaspoon
	Culturelle	Refrigerator	1 Capsule	Pull apart and mix with pear puree
	TMG	Med Box	1 Capsule	Pull apart and mix with pear puree
	Milk Thistle	Med Box	1 Capsule	Pull apart and mix with pear puree
	Enzyme with DPPIV	Med Box	1 Capsule	Pull apart and mix with pear puree
	CoQ 10	Med Box	1 Pill	Chewable
	Omega Rx	Freezer	1 teaspoon	Take out of freezer set on counter 10 minutes ~shake well pour
	AFTER BREAKFAST			
With Breakfast (8 AM)	Super NU-Thera with P5P	Med Box	1/2 Teaspoon	Takes straight off teaspoon
	DMSA (if "on day")	Kirkman Jar	4 capsules	Pull apart and mix with pears
	TWO HOURS LATER			

Set timer 45 minutes	Charcoal	Refrigerator	1 Capsule	After timer goes off ~ Pull apart and mix with pears
	THIRTY MINUTES LATER			
Set Timer 30 minutes	Charcoal	Refrigerator	1 Capsule	After timer goes off ~ Pull apart and mix with pears
Set timer 45 minutes				
	WITH LUNCH			
	Nystatin	Refrigerator	1 teaspoon	Take without food straight off teaspoon
Lunch (Noon to 1 PM)	Enzyme with DPPIV	Med Box	1 Capsule	Pull apart and mix with pear puree
	Super NU-Thera with P5P	Med Box	1/2 Tea-spoon	Takes straight off teaspoon
	DMSA (if "on day")	Kirkman Jar	4 capsules	Pull apart and mix with pears
	TWO HOURS LATER			
Set timer 45 minutes	Charcoal	Refrigerator	1 Capsule	After timer goes off ~ Pull apart and mix with pears
	THRITY MINUTES LATER			
Set Timer 30 minutes	Charcoal	Refrigerator	1 Capsule	After timer goes off ~ Pull apart and mix with pears
Set timer 45 minutes	WITH DINNER			
	Nystatin	Refrigerator	1 teaspoon	Take without food straight off teaspoon
Dinner or Snack (By 5 PM)	Enzyme with DPPIV	Med Box	1 Capsule	Pull apart and mix with pear puree
	Omega Rx	Freezer	1 teaspoon	Take out of freezer set on counter 10 minutes ~shake well pour
	Super NU-Thera with P5P	Med Box	1/2 Tea-spoon	Takes straight off teaspoon

	DMSA (if "on day")	Kirkman Jar	4 capsules	Pull apart and mix with pears
	AT BEDTIME			
Mid-Evening	Nystatin	Refrigerator	1 teaspoon	Take without food straight off teaspoon
Bed Time (By 8:00 PM)	Melatonin	Med Box	1/2 Pill~1.5mg	Dissolve in mouth before brushing teeth
	Zinc	Med Box	1 Capsule	Pull apart and mix with pear puree
	AFTER ASLEEP			
After Asleep	TTFD / Glutithione Cream	Closet Shelf	.5 cc each	Use glove put TTFD on bottom of foot, Glut. On forearm
	B 12 Shot	Med cupboard	.5 - .10 cc	put emla cream on area wait 1 hour then give shot through cream

"And let us not be weary in well doing: for in due season we shall reap, if we faint not" (Galatians 6:9).

REFLECTIONS FOR RECOVERY

∞ Discerning what, when, and who to use—take time to check your options, don't be afraid to interview those who will work with your child, and make sure personalities and goals match up well.

∞ Make sure you are part of your child's therapy so that it can continue after your appointments; don't just sit in a waiting room and read.

∞ Be respectful during requests of your therapists in explaining your desires to make greater progress, yet be flexible when times arise that it's best not to have distractions of others with a particular therapy session.

∞ Commit to dedicating yourself to apply everything you learn at home. Even if you are tired—short-term sacrifice is worth long-term gain!

My Thoughts

_____

_____

_____

Pearls for Others: "What can I do to help?"

∞ Offer to watch other children during tests, treatments, therapies.

∞ Help organize options, research therapies, treatments, doctors, make phone calls to gather information needed.

∞ Donate for a child's therapies/treatments, offer to hold a fundraiser/love offering in honor of the child (be sure family is comfortable before holding a fundraiser).

∞ Offer to go to appointments to help with the autistic child or take notes during doctor consultations.

∞ If you're an organizer, offer to organize medical and therapy home charts.

∞ Offer to learn the therapies given and help implement them at home.

∞ Encourage a family you know to persevere—send a note or write out scriptures/positive quotes for them to post around their home.

Ways I Commit to Help Someone I Know

_____

_____

_____

FAMILY MATTERS

Flexibility:
Not setting my affections on ideas or plans
which could be changed by God or others[6]

Learning flexibility has been a fruitful benefit for me. I have to admit that I much prefer to have all my ducks in a row, to plan out everything, and have life proceed according to those plans. But as Matthew 6:34 says, "Do not plan for tomorrow for you do not know what another day may bring forth" (NKJV). Our life just didn't ever seem to fit into the molds I had laid out in my mind! Though I battled it for years, I finally sought to observe others who seemed to take on life's changes in stride, those who could go with the flow and not get flustered when plans changed at the last minute. At times I felt I had more than life's share of challenges and changes, but in time, as I've learned to not count on things, I've been able to develop a deeper trust in the Lord and go with the flow more joyfully. Although I still plan ahead, I have learned to be open to life's adventures and changes along the way—I have experienced a renewed peace and contentment in my life from doing so, recognizing that I must be open and obedient to God's plans. "My soul wait thou only upon God: for my expectation is from him" (Psalm 62:5).

Flexibility while raising a child with autism is an absolute must. I recall the early years prior to understanding what was wrong with our son while we would be campaigning and at events, our son was most content to stand next to his grandpa, who was a U.S. Congressman at that time, and just hold his hand. It would always amaze me how he could be so good and just stand for hours at an event while grandpa talked with people. All the other children would be off playing together and would try to engage Richie to join them, but he would take no part. I later discovered that standing next to his grandpa gave him the security he needed in those crowded situations. Times like those we were very grateful for. For, In a moment, all that contentment could change and often did. When it was time to leave I would transfer his little hand from Grandpa's hand to my own and we would wait until most had left before trying to leave and put Richie in the car, a transition, in which he would have terrible fits, screaming, yelling, kicking, and biting. Just like with any transition in life for him without warning, he would react. We didn't understand why this happened at the time. All we knew is that more and more we were stressed to our limits when we went anywhere, never knowing what would set him off and what wouldn't, when he would be content to stand for hours and when he wouldn't.

During Rick's last campaign, and largest one for state representative, these sorts of behaviors had greatly increased. More and more, our sweet family campaigning days had to be cut short. The increased stress on Rick was insurmountable. None of us knew what was happening, nor why. Yet we had outside commitments. Places to be. Finally, we had to concede that we could no longer continue campaigning as a family. Rick continued to pursue his dreams; he sold his portion of the business and focused all time and energy on his campaign, running it from the lower level of our home. Times were trying as our son was diagnosed with autism during that campaign. It was during this campaign that I spent much time and energy researching what could be done for him. I would often stay up till wee hours after my studies for Richie, then I began working on campaign strategies, writing lit pieces, and praying that it would all work out.

We tried hiring babysitters to help us, but most never returned after the time spent behind our secluded walls of autism. Aside from some speech therapy, we had made little progress in learning how to handle or treat Richie's autism at that time. So, there really wasn't anyone who could handle all five children with the dynamics we had going. My mother continued to be a great source of help and support, running errands and picking up groceries for us and my dear Aunt Norma would regularly pick up Rick's ironing for me, since the dry cleaners was another *luxury* of the past we had to give up, replacing it with some of our initial costs of Richie's care. These types of help made a huge impact in assisting our family.

The campaign ran out of our home so it was a busy place to be, and we all helped as we could. Yet life was increasing to many levels of heightened stress. A campaign in itself is intense and experiences levels of stress; couple that with learning that your child has an untreatable disorder that is disrupting the entire family structure and you can imagine the hurricane that seemed always about to destroy everything within our family unit.

I recall desperately needing an updated family picture for our literature pieces. Out of desperation, I did fill a prescription that one of the psychiatrists gave us. All it did was make our son sleep twelve hours at night and then take a four to five-hour long nap during the day. He wanted to eat all the time when he was up and it did nothing to combat his symptoms; they were just limited due to him sleeping most of the time. It was during this trial month on medication that we finally made it to our photo session that had been repeatedly canceled due to us not being able to get Richie dressed and in the car. These photographers had done pictures for us in the past, but not since Richie's symptoms had heightened. Here we were with five children, ages one, two, four, six, and eight, a little dog and a cat (this is what I was still learning about dropping my plans and expectations!); anyhow, it still amazes me to this day how good our one and two-year-olds, the dog, and cat did—for it took over three hours to get a single shot where Richie would sit still. Needless to say, we were all exhausted after that photo shoot. I decided if none of the pictures came out, we would just skip the family picture on any literature. One picture did make it through though and was used. But to this day as I look upon that picture, I quickly recall where we were and how far we've come.

Finally, at nearing a deadline for the campaign, Rick recognized the fact that our family could not really continue at the pace we were in. Our son needed desperate measures with treatment, and it needed to be done quickly to gain the recovery we so desired for him. Rick hadn't begun his campaign in the usual way and support didn't seem to come easily. The decision Rick made to pull out of the race was a shock to many, including myself. Had autism stolen his dreams and his future?

As I watched him lose his own hope for the future, my heart ached for what was happening to our family. The thoughts of "why" surfaced over and over. What was next? What would we do? The bills were coming in by this point like a rushing tidal wave. Very few interventions we did for our son were covered by insurance. The little covered often was requested later to us in a bill as they reviewed and decided whatever tests/treatments we were doing for *autism* they didn't *recognize* as coverable.

This was likely because autism has been thought to be *untreatable.* I didn't know how to help my husband at that point. My time, energy, and strength was being sapped out of me daily with our home routine of *autism.* I really felt if I just focused on recovering our son, after he got better then everything else in life could get back to normal, and Rick could pursue his dreams of serving in office. We could be a family again who went out together serving in our community and church.

Life was consumed with everything I had to do for my son as I watched autism send its hurricane-strength winds into our home. Every aspect of life and hope dissipated. As I continued to watch the toll it was taking on our family, finances, and future, I was often haunted by that one doctor's words who wanted us to institutionalize our son, "You can't let one bad apple ruin the whole batch." Is that what was happening? Should we have listened to him? Then I would observe our son, who was beginning to make bits of progress in many different areas, and I would have to push any thoughts like those out of my mind. Striving forward, focusing on the future when he would be better was my determination.

I didn't cease praying and seeking God's Word daily. I couldn't as our future was looking more and more grim— that became my main hope and strength. Rick's defeat in politics affected his morale in pursuing something new after receding from the campaign, so without income, we had to make many changes. We recognized the fact that our beautiful home that Rick had built and together we added on to for our growing family had to be sold. We had to downsize and use that money to help pay all the bills. We cut back on everything. As the years passed, we lost all of our savings, sold our home, refinanced a new home to help pay the bills, and eventually ended up with our children on Medicare. How far we had come from; we used to have retirement, savings, lived debt-free, and sustained a comfortable lifestyle. We used to be a business and political family in the community, serving and caring for the needs of others. Now we were the extremely needy family, trying to survive.

As finances dissipated we had to make choices of how to continue with our son's treatments. This is how many families deal with trying to treat their children, knowing there are many things to help them but only to lack the financial means to provide these much-needed treatments. We finally had to cut out all the therapy, and I took that responsibility on my own at home. We maintained limited doctor's care and treated as much as we could. Rick spent hours upon hours on the phone with the insurance company, as they would agree to cover a bill and then later revoke that coverage. We didn't feel we could count on anything. We traveled to other states for IV treatments, and other special therapies we felt were a necessity, packing up our family and traveling to help our son on his road to recovery. Since Rick wasn't yet working again he was able to make many of these long-distance trips with us. However, the toll that took on him was great. Not only did he also have to live with and see the grips autism was making, he watched as our monies trying to recover Richie went out while none came in.

During one trip to New York to see his doctor and do some additional auditory and vision/light therapy only available there, Richie became very ill. It was Christmastime and we were there spending over $4,000 for the two weeks of specialized therapy, spending our Christmas holidays miles from home in a vacant (not a stitch of furniture) home. We were grateful for the home that was rent free and we made it a "camping" adventure for the kids, but this turned out to be one of those lost investments. Richie ended up having 106-degree fevers for days from a bacterial infection. Though he made it to some of his therapy treatments, we all knew that even when he was there, likely no progress was being made. He was just too sick. The insurance company had already pre-approved/paid for this therapy, and Richie was too ill to leave, so we stayed. He was treated with antibiotics, but we endured a challenging time and then had to reinstitute some of the past treatments to combat the instant yeast buildup from the antibiotics.

During this trip as I was talking with my mother on the phone one evening, her words became scrambled and confused. I asked her to wake my father, which seemed to take forever to get her to respond and wake him up. I later learned she had experienced a mini-stoke. I am grateful I was on the phone with her and able to help get my father to get her to the hospital, but again, this left me feeling helpless being miles away, unable to be with her. It seemed there were never-ending ways to pray and see the glass of life half full.

After arriving home we found that the insurance company decided to revoke coverage of the therapy that had been pre-approved from this New York trip. Seemed impossible for them to do, but they did it, and we had to pay. Rick, having to deal with these financial fights, was worn down further. Not certain what the future held or where he should focus on for himself and his career life was a challenge.

All during this time, the grips and stresses of autism in our family took its toll on our marriage. In fact, at one point it almost ended. We almost became one of the 80- 90% statistical marriages dealing with autism, which end in divorce. Just what that doctor had warned. But we worked hard to not allow that to happen. It was during this time, when those realities cropped into our lives, that I truly called upon friends and family for help and prayer for our marriage. Until this time, we had taken bits of help here and there. But no one really knew the depths to which we were struggling—until the day Rick decided he was no longer sure he wanted to be a part of our family at all.

I have learned that this is a very common fork in the road that marriages raising children with autism end up dealing with. Whether the marriage is strong or weak, Christian or not, in the beginning seems to make no difference. Facing these thoughts seems to creep into the minds of most marriages at some point throughout the process of raising a child with autism. Unfortunately, all too often these thoughts lead to actions for many and thus a broken marriage adds to the upheaval of the family already dealing with autism. Society needs to recognize the stress and strain that autism inflicts upon even the strongest and happiest of marriages.

Changing My Goals and Expectations

When that reality hit our home and I found myself alone with our five children for about four months, although some of the marital stresses dissipated with the separation and I didn't have to worry about Rick's frustration with the children, I continued to pursue reconciliation. Then my husband asked for a divorce. He had basically taken a few months' break from seeing our children and dealing with autism and found he liked it. Outside influences made it difficult for him to consider life by returning. It was at this point that it no longer mattered how many wrongs had occurred. My commitment to God and our marriage vows centralized my focus. Desiring to raise my children together with their father, my husband—I had to set aside hurts and pain, giving it all up to the Lord.

At this time there was one family in particular that reached out in a mighty way, investing in our future together. Although we had sought help here and there the months prior, no one had come alongside of us like the Burnard family did to help. Rick had returned to working and desired for me to join him at the accounting office where he was working so I could help contribute financially. Genesis 2:18 says, "The Lord God said, 'It is not good for the man to be alone. I will make a helper suited for him.'" So, I made the difficult decision to put three of our children (including Richie) in a public charter school, trusting God and letting go of my plans and goals for a season to honor my husband. Our other two children went to our dear friend's home, and she continued to tutor them in their schooling program and helped us by picking our other children up after school. It was a short-term, full-time commitment the Burnard family gave us as they honored all that we requested be done with our children and sought to help us in a way we couldn't have imagined. We will be forever grateful to them for their sacrifice and impact on our family's behalf. They learned Richie's dietary needs and agreed to our desires for all of our children in every area of life, sacrificing themselves and their time. We didn't even see eye to eye in all aspects spiritually, but with the respect they gave us honoring our beliefs, we felt confident and appreciated their willingness to help our family. This was a whole new life experience for all of us. I went from being a stay-at-home, homeschooling mother of five, implementing all of our son's therapies, to a working woman in a busy accounting firm, running an entire division of their office during tax season.

Though the change was difficult and another huge way I had to release my plans and expectations to the Lord, it was one of the things I did to obey and honor my husband. Rick and I drove to work together, worked often side by side, went to lunch together and as I let go of feeling guilty about what my homeschooling friends would think and anxious about our son's recovery, instead focusing on our marriage. It still wasn't easy as we soon learned that although this school had a program for our son, getting him there each morning was an hour-long battle and his regression from many of the strides he had made became increasingly evident. But we had committed until the end of that semester. Our marriage needed it. And I trusted God with it all.

When my husband's position was eliminated, we ended up leaving the accounting firm and beginning business together out of our home so that we could continue working together and spending lots of time together, which is why and how we originally fell in love. At the same time, Rick recognized the importance for us to bring our children home and allow all the benefits of homeschooling and home therapy to continue in our children's lives and bring our son's recovery back up to pace. Rick acknowledged Richie's needs and encouraged me in his recovery. What a huge difference it made.

The most important decisions and changes you can make in your family are to recognize the lack of balance that can occur during your pursuit of recovering your child from autism. In the effort to recover from autism, that which can tear your family apart, you can inadvertently begin severing it yourselves in the process of recovery. Between outside focus and distance from one's family avoiding the autism or inward focus and drive to recover your child and regain your lives, you can become out of balance. We must take care of ourselves and our spouse. If we are not caring for each other the way each one needs to be cared for, then we are setting ourselves up for destruction. No matter where you might be in your marriage, stop right now and evaluate it.

With autism, you can give in and allow it to destroy your family, or you can do what it takes to make it work, using all the challenges to build greater character within you. Don't wait for the other person. Take the steps now, yourself. Recognize balance and where it is or isn't happening for you. Get rid of pride. Focus on what could be. Focus on a future filled with happiness. What good will it be for your child and family if in the pursuit of recovery, in the end you wind up giving your child a new source of pain to deal with?

Perhaps you're thinking, *But you don't know the situation I'm in.* I don't, but what I do know is that we serve a mighty God who is quite capable of changing those situations. He's in the business of changing lives! What

I've personally found is that I must be willing to be the one to change first. I've learned that in *every* situation where people are concerned, there's always room for each person to make changes—even if it's simply being more patient, loving in their thoughts, and kind in their words. Gaining the ability to see the perspective of another is something I feel we can all benefit from. Become a better listener than talker. The list is endless and can be personalized for each situation. Take a minute to focus on self-change rather than self-fulfillment. Even when it doesn't make sense (it often didn't for me) and even when you can totally justify yourself (I often could, as did others around me), making your family work despite the past and what others may think can bring blessings from God.

Wherever you are, take a look at what it is that makes you feel loved. What made your spouse feel loved when you first fell in love? Ask questions of each other, take it to prayer, and figure out what it is that makes your spouse feel loved and unloved and then commit to loving them the way they need, while avoiding what makes them feel unloved. There are many great resources out there to help you on that process. Think you don't have time? Think it will ruin all your progress in helping your child recover? I believe you are wrong if both spouses are committed to God and doing what's right for their marriage. It will be the best thing you can do for *all* of your children. Staying in love—not just together, but in love—experiencing peace and harmony in your marriage, will be one of the greatest ingredients in bringing your child to recovery. But it must be both spouses committed to loving and caring for each other. It must be in a healthy way. There are times when we are led astray, believing things that are not true; in cases like these it's important to have discernment and not become an enabler to a spouse who is violating the true meaning of love and care. With everything, we must use discernment and seek wise counsel when needed.

REFLECTIONS FOR RECOVERY

∞ Are you willing to be the first one to change? To make a commitment to repair severed relationships in your family, with a spouse, child, or other loved one?

∞ How can you add members of your family into your autistic child's life?

∞ Are you willing to forgo some of your therapy for a period to have time to invest into your family?

∞ Is there someone else who could take your children giving you time for planning a date night with your spouse or taking a special time out with another child?

∞ Make your family time fun time. If it's hard to do in your home then go for a walk, go to a park, or someone's home where there is joy.

∞ You must experience joy to give and receive it. To recognize what it is and if it's missing, surround yourself with others who have it! Love your children and your spouse—love covers a multitude of sins!

∞ Enlist family or friends to help with your children so that you can take *regular* date nights together.

∞ Don't set exceedingly high expectations on your family or things that perhaps used to be more important, like a perfectly organized home or manicured lawn. In the end, most people are always more concerned about the relationships in their lives. Make the investment into those relationships a priority.

∞ Remember: short-term sacrifice for long-term gain!

My Personal Thoughts

_____

_____

_____

Pearls for Others: "What can I do to help?"

∞ Give a list of special "outings" that would work with the special-needs child and offer to go along and help.

∞ Offer to watch children on a regular basis for parents to go out together. A date they can count on.

∞ Go to their home to learn how best to care for the special-needs child so parents can relax and enjoy while gone.

∞ Play/spend time with a family's special needs child at family gatherings. My brother used to do this for me during holidays and he genuinely would get down and play with Richie. That little bit of "down time" for me made such a difference to enjoy the gathering and relax.

∞ Offer an overnight babysitting for the parents to have a really special time together. If funds are low, just exchange houses and leave candles and soft music playing, and perhaps dinner or carryout at your home for them to enjoy and feel special and nurtured—and offer to go grocery shopping or run errands prior to your arrival so that they can leave and relax, rather than feeling like they have to use their date time to "catch up on everything."

Ways I Commit To Help Someone I Know

_____

_____

_____

ENDURING THE SEASON

Endurance:
The inward strength to withstand
stress to accomplish God's best[7]

The opposite of endurance is giving up! Endurance is the inward strength to withstand stress to accomplish God's best. Where does this strength come from and how do we know what to do to achieve God's best? For me, it was trusting totally in a Savior who understood every aspect of what I was dealing with on a daily, moment-by-moment basis. Maintaining faith was my goal and greatest objective. During those very trying weeks, months, and years I can honestly look back and see that the strength from within to keep going, persevering when all aspects of life looked too grim for hope came completely from my faith in God. But I didn't always have that kind of faith.

First Florida Move

Shortly after our first daughter was born, we moved from our hometown to Ft. Lauderdale so my husband could assist in family business there. Since our new little baby was extremely inflicted with colic and our Michigan season was turning cold, rainy, and dreary the thought of sunny Florida was well received. My father-in-law took us to church that Easter to Coral Ridge Presbyterian Church in Fort Lauderdale. Although I had grown up as an avid churchgoer and would have called myself a Christian, I was soon to realize that I never truly knew or understood the deeper meaning behind being a Christian. After our initial outing to Coral Ridge, Rick and I continued attending church there, as we were enthralled with Dr. D. James Kennedy's ability to preach the Word of God. Yet, still something was missing in my life.

Eternal Life

Then one day, Dr. Kennedy's wife, Anne, came to visit our family. I thought it was a traditional time for them to welcome us as ongoing visitors to the church. But that night proved to be a turning point that redirected and would ultimately shape the rest of the course of my life. In just two short questions, Anne knew what it was I was missing in my life—a true relationship with Jesus Christ, the one who came to earth to pay the penalty for my sins to secure a place for me in heaven. One who suffered in an ever-plausible way and promised never to leave me nor forsake me. This visit and those questions were a result of an international ministry called Evangelism Explosion that Dr. Kennedy founded.

The questions. First, she asked if I knew for certain that if I died that night that I would go to heaven. Well, that was a question I had asked numerous others my entire life. Since I can remember talking, I can remember asking people that very question! I had such a fear of death and of those I loved dying that at times the answer to that question became almost an obsessive thought for me as a child. My answers revolved around hope. I sure did hope, but I shared that through my research in questioning others through college and beyond, I never did find that one could know for sure they would go to heaven.

The second question was, "If I were to die tonight and stand before God, and He were to ask, 'Why should I let you into my heaven?' What would I say?" Of course my hair went up on my back just thinking such a thought, so I quickly relinquished many possible ways I felt I had been a fairly good person and again hoped that would be enough to get me into heaven.

Then she shared with me the greatest news I had ever heard. The Bible does say that you *can* know for certain that you are going to heaven. She proceeded to share with me how to know that and what I needed to do by simply praying from my heart, acknowledging that I am a sinner, and totally putting my trust and faith into Christ, who came for the sole purpose of reserving a place for me in heaven. I made that decision that night and my life has never been the same since.

Now, that definitely didn't mean that I no longer had any problems! In fact, most of my life's most difficult challenges have occurred since that time. But my personal reflection is not what's happened in my life, but rather where I might be (or the rest of my family) had I not made that important decision that night and surrendered my life to Christ. Because of that decision when life was totally out of control, when there was darkness everywhere, and when hope seemed a distant past, I endured. I know now it wasn't really me and my strength, just like it wasn't me and my works that could get me into heaven. But it was through Christ, who strengthened me, that giving up on autism didn't happen.

Dr. Kennedy and his wife, Anne, immediately took me under their wing and discipled me through to this day. They were always available to me when I had a question or concern. Anne and I became prayer partners and after our move back to Michigan, she continued to keep in touch with me. Thanks to a few years later and the development of e-mail we were able to keep in constant contact with each other. I have treasured their friendship, love, and example for the Lord all these years.

I had begun to read my Bible faithfully, and by the grace of God, He taught me how to trust in Him through all the toils and troubles I would encounter. If you are out there hanging onto your own strength or wondering for certain where you are going to end up when you die, I encourage you to seek the resources in the back of this book on "Going to Heaven" and surrender your life to the One who cares most for you.

Cancer

Not only did I gain greater insights into having faith, trusting in prayer, and gleaning wisdom, but I also had others around me who exampled for me how to endure when times were tough or the future seemed hopeless. My mother suffered with non-hodgekins lymphoma back when most everyone was dying from it. She battled it and won! Got back into life, and within about six months it returned fiercer than before. My mother's physical strength was less than the first battle; she seemed more fragile and weak. But doctors opted to aggressively treat her, as they knew her chances for survival were slim. Many trying months into treatments, in and out of the hospital, having veins collapse and enduring unbelievably painful side effects from the chemo, she ended up in ICU on death's door. The chemo was killing her now! We were told that she would not survive. Her blood was black, without oxygen her lungs were collapsing, she was on a ventilator and every other hook up imaginable.

Through it all, she never gave up, never complained, never got angry. My father was a testimony of faithfulness and dedication, as he did whatever it took to be by her side throughout all those months and years. He was always there. As a bedside support, his example taught me much about what commitment and dedication to family and marriage really meant. I am so grateful to parents who gave me those examples of commitment through difficult and trying times. Their dedication to marriage has always been a huge testimony and example for me to live out.

Within a week of being in ICU and told she would not get off the ventilator, that she would soon die, my mother was up sitting in a chair. Truly an answer to many prayers and a reflection of love and dedication that stood by her side and encouraged her, giving her reason to fight and live were her family and friends. Though long and tough was the battle, she survived. However, not without many continuing side effects from the chemotherapy. Effects that have been very severe at times, adding daily pain and discomfort to her life, but she feels blessed. And after twenty years of remission, she continues to look at those painful and annoying side effects as daily reminders to be thankful that she is still here, able to be a part of her two children getting married and the births and raising of her eight grandchildren. She has been a tremendous testimony of a meek and quiet spirit to me. Not to mention all of the help she has lent over the years, and I will be eternally grateful to God that He has spared her life for so long and given me a mother who has taught me, by example, such valuable lessons in life about not giving up and enduring the season, and for my father's example of putting family first no matter what the cost. They now enjoy retired life together and are more active, bike riding, golfing, and serving in their community than most retired people I know!

They have always lent a helping hand to anyone in need. I recall a time when my parents had moved about an hour from the city I grew up in while I was in college. Home for summer break, I was returning from work one evening to find a carload of my friends driving out of our road. I apologized for missing their visit and found that they had spent the afternoon with my parents who they had come to visit! Everyone missed my parents when they moved away. That's the loving, kind parents I'm grateful to have. So many people have been blessed by their genuine love and hospitality, a value that I, too, cherish.

Fire in The House!

Another fine example of endurance for me has been through my father-in-law. He did not have an especially easy life. He worked hard and, as a result, ended up in that eighty percent of self-made millionaires in America through business entrepreneurship. But he didn't stop there; he had a commitment to sacrifice and giving back to the community, which supported him during his growing years. So, serving in Congress and volunteering in the community extensively while extending continual hospitality, he and his wife, Katie, were an example in our community of people who opened their home to anyone in need or for any way to help a good cause. Their home was like a museum to me, a homey, inviting, and comfortable one in which pictures of presidents and other great officials lined the walls. Documents from our forefathers displayed the roots of our country. Books of all sorts were readily available resources on the shelves.

His home was often filled with people from all over the world, enjoying themselves as they were graciously served. We enjoyed wedding showers, baby showers, family weddings, fun sleepovers, and many other family functions in their home.

Following a bad thunderstorm causing multiple power outages, my daughters and I had been given a local ice cream parlor's huge container of moosetracks ice cream, which would have melted without our rescue. We couldn't bring it home due to Richie's special diet, so we brought it to Grandpa Chrysler and Grandma Katie's house since we knew they had a freezer to fit it and they also loved ice cream! We visited that evening for a midnight ice cream party in their somewhat darkened home, which suffered partial power failure due to the previous storm. It was great fun since we rarely enjoyed *real* ice cream. The girls even asked to spend the night. But late into the night we all ventured home. The next morning about 5:30, I got a call from my father-in-law, and his words were simple, "Kristi, the house is burning down." Since we lived right across the street, I looked out the window in disbelief and could see the flames far above the forty to fifty foot trees between our homes. We quickly ran across to find Dad and Katie with their two dogs on the lawn near the lake, watching their home engulf in flames. Their 12,000 square foot home continued to burn for three days. Despite the efforts of fire officials from six areas, it was hopeless to stop the fire. How grateful we were that no one was hurt or killed. Apparently there was a power surge going into their home as a result of the storm and power outages that the electrical department had not yet detected. This surge started a fire in an electric door that got its grip throughout the night between the second and third floor trusses. Truly it was a miracle that they woke up and got out just in time. Minutes later and we would have lost them along with the house.

As tragic and momumentous as that fire was, something much greater has cemented itself into my mind from that experience. The night after the fire had completely encapsulated the house and there was no hope for retrieving anything, my father-in-law came over to our home. I was reading a bedtime story to our children who had been so full of questions of what Grandma and Grandpa Chrysler were going to do and how sad they all were for the loss of so much. When he entered the room, he quietly sat down, having us complete our story time. Then came the questions from the children to him…and in his calm and sweet manner, he just told them his story that life is like eating an elephant, you just have to take one small bite at a time. And he also related that when you get lemons, just focus on making lemonade out of them. About that time, our middle son, who about was about four years old at that time, came into the room carrying a briefcase. A few days earlier, he had been playing with one of grandpa's briefcases, as he had a fixation on collecting cases of any kind to hold all of his collection of treasures. Grandpa Chrysler had told him to just take it home for his *treasure collection* since he had many other briefcases he could use. Now at that precious moment after their fire, John proceeded to give it back to Grandpa, saying, "I think you might need this more than I do now, Grandpa, you don't have any left after the fire."

With tears in our eyes, our hearts aching, Grandpa's

response that day was, "Now you see, children, I can go to work. Life is like an elephant, you can only do it one bite at a time. And if you don't worry about the little problems, there will be no big problems. That's the first step. Just remember, whatever happens to you, you just take it one step at a time, like eating that elephant." That moment froze in time for me, one that I would reflect on often when I felt overwhelmed and defeated ready to give up.

I never saw or heard him get angry or upset, even once, about their losses. Those were all *things* he would say. But in reality they were irreplaceable reflections of his life's investments that would have devastated most people I know. His and Katie's testimony of pressing forward and not looking back was an example I would often reflect on, much like my own mother and father's example of love, dedication, and endurance.

In my situation I realized that I had to give up my own expectations, for myself, my husband, the therapists, and doctors. Our son's recovery was a great hope and desire, but I tried to stay focused on the bite I was taking, rather than on the entire elephant that would consume me. In doing this, I was more able to work with everyone involved in my son's treatments, not holding any one person to perfection and cure. *I had to come to a reality that what worked for one child may or may not give progress to my own son.* So much of what we were doing was trial and experimental in use for autism, and we learned there is definitely not a one-size-fits-all treatment for autism. But how grateful we were to have something to try when so many told us there was no treatment. As a result, we found that all these *trial treatments* brought our son out of autism into recovery.

Getting through it all took organization of every area of our lives. Simplifying every possible aspect of life was essential. Routine and lack of change was very important to prevent Richie's breakdowns from occurring and disrupting the demanding intervention that needed to be accomplished daily. This was new way of life for us from being so used to political and campaign life, which seemed to turn with the wind and was busy and filled with adventure and excitement. Faced with being home-bound, our excitement and adventure replaced itself from fancy dinners, functions, and people to hikes in our back fields and woods, just to escape the walls of our home yet protect us from the outside dangers and judgment of autism. Almost daily the children and I ventured outside to help relieve the stresses of housebound life filled with ongoing home therapy intermixed with continual meltdowns. I have to admit, although our parents set examples of greatness and endurance for us, I wasn't always without complaint, sorrow, and at times, despair. I tried to hide it, but in my heart I did have to battle those feelings on occasion.

At times it was hard for me to accept help. When asked if I needed anything, I often couldn't come up with anything that seemed worth another person's time to help with. I was so consumed with *doing autism,* I often couldn't collect my thoughts to organize what someone else could do to help! Autism does that to you—ask any mother in the depths of it. There were times when I could hardly get along with just maintaining the simplest tasks of running our home. Autism has a way of invading every area of a family's life and leaving us prone to any number of emotions. Preparing for each day of therapy would result in many battles to be won with Richie. Every aspect of clothing was terribly difficult for him, with socks and shoes being the hardest due to sensory overload he experienced. We would always leave socks and shoes for when we arrived at each appointment. And there were times they simply stayed in the car, and I carried my son. I was grateful we had a heated garage that kept him warm getting into the car each time we left the house. Another battle that often demanded up to thirty extra minutes of time was getting into a seat and buckling the seatbelt. I would plan about one and a half hours to get him dressed and in the car buckled and safe and then plan an additional half hour to try to get his socks and shoes on once we arrived at our destination. Since living in Michigan, most of our weather was not conducive to shorts, T-shirts, and bare feet. This would result in a single half-hour therapy appointment taking us two to three hours of work getting there, depending on the distance from our home! (That didn't include getting my other four children ready!) And we did this almost every day for a season of life. Everything else in life seemed to be rushing by me as I fixated on how to achieve each moment-by-moment task with Richie.

We could no longer attend church, which was a real disappointment for me. I was already without any social outings and then my faith and endurance was left up to me to study and pray on my own. I did rely on tapes of sermons and watching Dr. Kennedy televised on the Coral Ridge Hour. I'm so grateful I had those resources. The isolation a mother of an autistic child feels at times is beyond understanding, unless, of course, you are one. Thus why members of support groups amongst parents with autistic children seem to instantly bond. It amazes me when I travel to conferences and speak with other parents dealing with autism what a connection we all instantly have, simply through facing the same challenges/experiences daily.

As time went on, though, we began to see bits and pieces of progress due to these biomedical treatments and various therapies, though nothing came to us in leaps and bounds and it often seemed we would take one step forward in one area, like speech, and then go two steps back in sensory issues. It was a rollercoaster that never let you get off to ground yourself. In a whirlwind of life, one day rolled into another. My faith was great and growing, but aspects of life all around me were falling apart, but I was too busy trying to keep my focus on the ride I was on.

I honestly was too busy battling autism, working with my son and other children daily, to worry too much about my own health. But it did wear on me. I learned pushing past daily pain and exhaustion had to be a mind-set during much of this season (since I still suffered from lupus, which flared at times). Sure, I felt like giving up many times, I felt like not getting out of bed, but there was no one else to do my *job.* "Keep pressing on"—I had to repeat those words often in my mind so I wouldn't lose my endurance to lupus, or anything else. As I reflect, the mind-set likened that of an Olympic trainer, constantly keeping your eye on the goal. Doing the best you can. Not giving up. Pushing past the pain. Enduring. Focus. Focus. Focus. Never give up.

Though there's been no ceremony or lighted torch to carry with our win of recovery—my son and my family are Olympic Gold Medals for me. Having Richie back and recovered while maintaining all my family's needs—that's been our quiet celebration of victory.

REFLECTIONS FOR RECOVERY

∞ It's raining; as a matter of fact, it's rainy season in England. The weather is not due to change for weeks. Are you going to resort to staying in, or will you get out your galoshes, raincoat, and umbrella and go out and do what you have to do? Treating autism is much the same way. Get on what you need and then move forward in some small way. Don't wait for the sun to shine; you need to go and search out your own rainbows.

∞ Are you focusing on your cup being half full or half empty? One will encourage you, and the other will discourage you.

∞ Where is your faith? If you're not sure, see "Going to Heaven" in the appendix.

∞ Again, if you've not given up but things have gotten out of balance and you're trying to eat the whole elephant, step back, reevaluate your marriage and family relationships, do what it takes to put things back into order. Do it before it's too late. Don't think those are not pieces in your child's road to recovery. They could be the very pieces still missing.

∞ Endurance is a must. Figure out what motivates you, then set it before you daily to succeed.

My Personal Thoughts

_____

_____

_____

Pearls for Others: "What can I do to help?"

∞ Pray often for a family and child (see appendix: Prayer of Destiny).

∞ Offer to watch an autistic child during alternating church services so that rest of family can attend church and make it a special time for the special needs child as well.

∞ Offer to take other children to special church and community programs with your own family.

∞ Offer to help a special-needs child maintain diet and other special needs at church, family outings, other community events, or school.

∞ Offer to go with a special-needs child if they are able to be in a class but not without an aid.

∞ Send encouraging cards and notes.

∞ Drop off flowers.

∞ Encourage a family to endure to the end and be their strength when times are tough. Like a good coach, give them that loving nudge to keep pressing on when needed.

Ways I Commit To Help Someone I Know

_____

_____

_____

HARVESTING FRUIT
THROUGH HOMESCHOOLING

Humility:
Recognizing that it is actually God and others
who are responsible for the achievements in my life[8]

Homeschooling our children was one of the best decisions our family made to help our son come to full recovery, even though we didn't realize it at the time. Though I know homeschooling may not seem possible for everyone, if you've not considered it and your current schooling situation doesn't seem to be producing the fruit you desire for your children, it might be worth looking into. I admit, for me it was something I did try to get out of doing for Richie on occasion. I kept wondering if I was doing an acceptable job educating him, if I was truly equipped to handle his special needs. But the fruit I saw produced in all of our children kept me going, as I trusted the Lord to guide me. If I had only realized how beneficial homeschooling actually was for all of our children while recovering Richie from autism, then I would have saved myself endless hours of wondering and researching educational options for him.

Though I excitedly began home educating our children from the start, my doubt crept in with Richie's behaviors taking on so much of my time and energy coupled with feeling that I wasn't making adequate progress at all with him, caused me to look into every conceivable option possible. I checked into special education programs, special schools for autism, private and public possibilities. With my husband's encouragement, I even moved from Michigan to Florida, planning for Richie to attend a special school for autism that incorporated all his therapies and diet into his school day. I spoke with the school's director and had everything approved prior to our move. I was excited about this opportunity to give Richie this special education and the rest of us a little break.

I arrived in Florida with my five children. We got settled in a home we planned to be at for the next six months and set off to the school, only to be told he was still "too bad behaviorally with autism" to be accepted. A school for autism said he was still too bad and yet we had come so far and he was doing much better than he had been. I realized as far as we had come, we were nowhere near recovered. So back I moved to Michigan, trying what I could. But each time there was something about each program that didn't fit well or seem right. Although I often doubted myself, I pressed on, taking one bite at a time of that enormous elephant called autism.

Continuing by plugging along as best as I knew how, I incorporated all of his therapies into his daily routines adjusting our schedule around what would work for everyone. I was able to focus greatly on his social skills, since I was almost always around him and training the other children as well; teaching him how to respond to every possible situation became incorporated into our school and life routine. It seemed so unnatural to *teach him* how to be sad and when it was appropriate, how to laugh and when things were funny. Every aspect of *normal* human emotion we taught him daily. When he didn't respond properly, we went back and replayed the situation so that he could learn how to respond properly. Since we were always together, rarely did a situation occur that I wasn't made aware of so we could go back and *replay it.* We even had daily *practice time* where we made up situations and "acted out how to respond" when someone got hurt, made a joke, etc. I used social stories to help incorporate these *normal* skills into Richie's learning. We practiced doing everything at home, which someday

I hoped to be able to accomplish outside of the home. We practiced going shopping (around the kitchen table, I would set up *store* with all kinds of tempting goodies and we would practice walking around them without touching or having tantrums). We practiced accepting the answer "no" and how to respond. We sat in chairs in a circle and *played church,* learning how to sit still, be quiet, sing hymns and respond to certain cues. I began to see very slow and gradual progress, never knowing if it would become automatic for him. If it ever did, it would allow us the opportunity to incorporate our family into typical outings.

By always incorporating his siblings, the younger boys learned *how to act properly* right along with him. I just used all the same therapies and methods I was learning and developing for Richie for them as well and praised them when they responded correctly. Consequently, they were being taught as toddlers proper responses while I worked to undo all the inappropriate behavior they mimicked from their older brother, so that began to work as they each *caught on.* It became exciting as the children would be playing together, and one would joyfully come running to me recapping an event in which Richie used the proper social cues. They would be excited and praising him, telling me the story. He began to glow during these times, and it seemed he wanted to please. He just needed much more help to learn how to appropriately. And he gained greater patience as he endured meltdowns, and we learned how to teach him better ways to cope and respond. With the consistency of his siblings and me working diligently with him in every area of life—from school, to play, to family life—he couldn't help but begin to *get it*. I believe he caught on quicker and more obligingly from his siblings (being at closer ages to him) than from all the adult therapists and myself.

As hard and sacrificial as it was at times for all of us, I've asked my children, and none of us would do it differently if to do it all over again. All of our children learned the meaning and value of self-sacrifice at a young age. Of hard work with little progress. Of flexibility coupled with love. They learned and continue to reflect on the importance of family first. Relationship skills have been developed, especially by our older children, that may never have been touched normally until much later in life. The choices we made to homeschool everyone and include each of the children into Richie's life and his process of recovery has given them greater life and relational skills than I had at their ages. And we all stayed connected with each other, rather than disconnecting with everyone having a separate agenda going their separate ways. My children are still youngsters, and we are all working to improve our weaknesses. But how great it is to see our children learn and mature—there's no greater joy!

I learned that many great people in history were home educated, such as Abraham Lincoln and Thomas Jefferson, just to name a couple. And even in times past, school was a place our children learned respect and relationship skills, incorporating many different ages together. I recognize home-educated children in our society are the minority, yet I have observed how many of these children are growing into well-educated young people and adults, winning many academic awards and achievements while growing in leadership and character. Personally, I feel it's the social skills our home-educated children learn that makes it one of the preferred choices for many who make that sacrifice to do so, contrary to what much of society perceives with homeschooled children. Teaching our children to be best of friends, becoming a parent who can discipline ourselves to require honor and respect of our children and teens, while maintaining mutual love and respect is a feat for most of us parents. But as a homeschooling parent, you're not going to be able to slack on such responsibilities, since you're around your children all the time. There's no escape of sending your kids off to school many hours each day for a "break," blaming their poor behaviors on the kids they are around all day. I believe that mere fact would render me slothful in being as disciplined and consistent as I need to be as a parent and as I needed to be with Richie.

Homeschooling is a 24/7 occupation with no lunch breaks, coffee breaks, or sick days. We don't tend to ever take a day *off* or take a *break!* But the blessings of experiencing each new stride in each child's life, being right there to encourage them, love them, and listen to them is far too great of an opportunity to miss out on. Not to mention our days off and breaks are now spent together enjoying the loving relationships that homeschooling helped develop.

I am grateful for those who encouraged us along the way not to give up or give in to outside pressures, especially with schooling Richie at home. And I'm grateful to God who knew best, that He didn't allow other schooling options to work out for Richie when I was discouraged and seeking other solutions, easier solutions. It was ultimately through His strength that I was able to succeed in this endeavor of homeschooling my five children, one with autism. I've found that God often puts me into situations that seem impossible (like writing this book!), and without Him I realize they are! But getting on my knees and recognizing I can do nothing apart from Him and His strength has humbled me and brought me into a closer relationship with Him.

This choice to homeschool has been another large collection of puzzle pieces that has worked together to complete the picture of Richie's recovery. Whether that is the direction of your life or another means is for your child, be sure that you play an active and intimate role in every aspect of your children's lives. Know what they are studying, who their friends are, and what they are like. Spend time with them and *listen* to them. Make *time* for them. And lots of it! So often in the busyness of life we don't realize we are skating along, only half hearing what our children are saying. But our children usually know when they don't have our full attention, that we're preoccupied with something else, which communicates to them their level of importance or lack thereof in our lives. What do we want them to think is more important in life? People, or all those things that distract us from our children? Our special-needs children, especially, need our ears, our hearts, and our love—not just our correction. And their siblings do equally as well. We need to be our children's number-one cheerleader, encouraging them and praising them along the way of life. No matter where they are educated, just commit to being an integral part of this important time in their lives. They need to know they can trust us with anything. But it's up to us to earn that trust by being there for them. Teaching them and training them right from wrong, but loving them along the way. Be disciplined and consistent. Love your children so they feel it. Be available.

Creative Methods That Worked

Along our road to educating our special-needs child I learned that each of my children was special and unique in their learning style. What worked for one didn't always produce the same results for another. The wonderful aspect of homeschooling is that you have the flexibility to adjust your curriculum to meet the needs and produce the best results possible for each individual child.

Learning some techniques from the Montessori Method of teaching became a valuable resource for me when Richie was young. Having a dear friend, Kathy Moorehouse, who ran a wonderful Christian Montessori school, we attended together for about three months and gleaned all we could from her teaching methods, along with a heavy dose of studying these methods from books and research. Not all Montessori schools are the same and follow the original guidelines set, so I recommend if you're interested in learning more to check out books by Maria Montessori who developed this method of teaching children. She was given the awesome task of taking the then-called "street urchins" off the alleys of England and making something good of them, many of them homeless and with a variety of issues, what we would call today as autistic, retarded, ADHD, ADD, bipolar, etc. In her tasks she developed a method of teaching them that was phenomenal, producing caring, creative, capable children who grew up with the ability to learn and be productive in society.

We brought home many of the techniques I learned

and studied on my own and used a variety of the resources, which gave Richie a hands-on approach to learning. I also attended many workshops for special-needs teachers, learning everything I could from teaching special learners how to read, to write, behavior intervention, etc. I traveled everywhere researching and studying. If there was something I could attend and glean from, I made every effort to be there. I became a student myself of educating special-needs children. I also attended workshops for speech therapy, OT, PT, sensory integration therapy, etc. I asked all of Richie's therapists to give us *homework* that I could use in our homeschool program.

Applying every aspect of life to learning and embarking on a *family education* rather than a school program for my children became the focus for our home. During those early years, Richie's attention and hyperness would be such a distraction it seemed impossible to implement academics. I had to get creative. Actually, to be honest, I prayed often for wisdom and creativity in schooling him along with the others. "Commit thy works unto the Lord, and thy thoughts shall be established" (Proverbs 16:3). An answer to prayer came when I learned that since writing was such an effort for Richie, that itself was a challenging OT discipline, so I prayed for creativity to get his work accomplished. To make him sit in a chair and write his math answers only proved timely and trying for all of us while the objective of learning math was never achieved. So, with insight from God, we ended up outside with the basketball and hoop (which incorporated PT, academics, and phys-ed together!); we would bounce the ball and say a series of math facts to win a chance at shooting a basket. Then we would move to sidewalk chalk and jump on the problems I would write out, as we said them and physically integrated them. My younger boys would join us and to my surprise, the basketball bouncing during free time usually accompanied someone chanting "2, 4, 6, 8, 10…shoot a basket!" even when they weren't doing "school" and were just out having fun! So inadvertently the younger siblings learned much without realizing it or with any *formal schooling*, which is common in the homeschooling environment.

I also implemented the use of documentary educational videos in his learning. We had canceled cable to eliminate easy access to television, as that would quickly become another source of fixation for Richie. I utilized every kind of educational video I could to implement areas of his academics. However, I could lock away these videos and only allow delegated amounts of time or else he could spend an entire day watching documentaries. We realized that he was very good memorizing with visual/auditory cues, so the use of fact-filled visual educational or documentary videos led him to gain and retain insight in many areas of educational statistics, facts, and dates the rest of us would soon forget. And he enjoyed every minute of learning this way and teaching the rest of us along the way.

His need for visual learning to accompany much of his studies was a revelation during his bedtime meltdowns. I had always read a chapter out of a chapter book without pictures each night before bed. Prior to Richie's ability to communicate, I would have to try to get him to sleep prior to reading, as he would always have a meltdown. Our oldest daughter realized that without having a picture to look at, Richie would break down because early on he lacked the ability to *imagine* what was being read. So she thought to create a picture book she presented to him as I read. She had copied/drawn pictures depicting the different people and places I was reading about. She pointed to the pictures she created to illustrate the story I was reading. He eventually learned to create the pictures of what was being read in his own mind and now is my number-one fan of our reading time before bed.

All these areas we dealt with were like bits of detective work. A mystery uncovering the source of the breakdown. Then creatively seeking measures to combat, deter, and ultimately reverse the meltdown. My girls became experts at anticipating triggers and interceding for him. This eventually led us to better identify areas of weakness for him and equip him with the tools necessary to master additional challenges, preventing his meltdowns. Understanding these areas allowed us to solicit help from other families, even just boys a few years older who would play basketball with math facts or play *pretend* with Playmobile so Richie could continue to have nonstop one-on-one interaction. We *created* one-on-one *peer therapists* for him, since at that time where we lived there were no professional therapists we could use or afford.

One valuable addition I learned from one therapist was to make tapes that Richie would listen to each night. We learned the importance of praising your children twenty praises for every one correction. Since Richie needed so much correction/redirection it seemed impossible to ever come close to that ratio. So we began to make tapes of affirmations. And there were many—he was our son, God made him, he was a gift to us, he was important, he was needed, he was loved, he was special, he was musical, and so on. After putting him to bed I would play this repeating tape of affirmations for him until we resigned. So, from our voices each night he would hear us reaffirm how special, loved, and important he was. Even if it had been a tremendously difficult day, he would end it with positive affirmations of who he was and what he could be from those of us who also had to correct and re-direct, nonstop during the day. We also did this for our other children and worked hard to try to keep the focus as equal as possible by including them with everything—even affirmation tapes! They were trooper as well!

To be honest, I'm not sure I could have done all I did without schooling my children at home—though there were times that I felt if only I wasn't, then I'd have the time to…But in reflection of the years thus far, I realize all the flexibility in my schedule allowed me to fit all the therapies, interventions, etc., in a way that best suited our family dynamics, rather than always working around so many other pre-scheduled commitments and outside routines. And our children were continually drawn together.

Was it a sacrifice? Of course it was. But so was getting my children ready every morning and taking them to school during the semester I was employed with my husband outside the home. Then dealing with situations out of my control, such as dietary infractions, inappropriate behaviors picked up, poor language copied, etc. were just a few issues I dealt with while the children were away at school. Everything in life has some sort of sacrifice. The real question is whether your sacrifice is producing positive or negative results. I have such close-knit bonds with all my children and they do with each other, so for me I can reflect that the sacrifice of certain things to home educate my children is far worth any gain to choose other options of education. I believe we each need to seek out what is best for our family.

The children were all a part of the recovery process. Each life has been touched and has grown and developed character qualities that I don't believe would have been developed without our being together through this process. Having everyone intertwined also allowed me to better know, understand, and deal with issues for our other four children, recognizing they each had needs of their own. By spending the time necessary so they would not feel abandoned or resentful due to the time it took for Richie's needs to be met, I scheduled "special alone times" with each of the children, and we continue to do that to this day. Whether it is a special story time, talk time, or outing for a treat, we take time together individually that was just not possible for me when they all went away to school.

The scrutiny of homeschooling, was it worth it? Many therapists at first looked down on me when they would learn that I was homeschooling all of my children, especially my special-needs son. I'm sure they questioned my qualifications. However, when they saw the implementation of their therapy in my daily lessons, learned how eager I was to gain insight into teaching my son and gleaning from their expertise, as well as including all the children to make it a part of Richie's life, the results spoke for themselves. In the end, most all of our therapists became fans of homeschooling, helping us develop therapy into his curriculum and were a tremendous support to our family.

At one point during a very busy time of transitioning and moving two times in a few months, I hired an ABA therapist to come to our home and implement Richie's homeschooling program for me so I had time to clean out and pack boxes for yet another move. I'm not too sure what she thought of the idea at first, but by the time we moved we were all sad she couldn't move across many states and continue with us, since she had become a fan of homeschooling and had made great progress with Richie! She did come a spend a couple weeks with us, as there was a special autism school open where Richie could go for all his therapy. She went and observed the school and all they had to offer Richie just from the therapy perspective. When she returned her advice was to keep him home and continue doing what we had been, implementing everything ourselves. She truly felt he would regress in the other environment and she had firsthand seen how much he progressed in just the few months she implemented his homeschooling program. Although it wasn't always easy, I'm so glad we followed her advice. Erica Blackbourne was another huge piece for advising and encouraging us toward Richie's recovery.

Manipulation. Learned behaviors. These are just a couple of the ways that autism can play a role, even into recovery. As I learned, the better Richie improved in various areas of life and the less trouble he had controlling himself. As a natural born boy with wants and desires, he would at times seem to flip back to some autistic behavior. I had to continually discern what was autism and what was disobedience at that point and quickly apply appropriate discipline. As his communication improved we talked about that fact and one day he laughed and said, it's like a comedian I saw mom. He said, "Laundry? I can't do laundry, I don't know how, I'm autistic!" This is where the closeness that homeschooling allowed me to have in his life gave me insight into his recovery and the ways that he inadvertently used autistic behaviors (a tantrum, etc.) to try to get what he wanted on his road to recovery.

There was a day when that was real, now I accept *none* of it! Even if he slips and eats something he knows he shouldn't (since he does have to remain GFCF) he knows he best gain self-control of hyperactivity and cope in appropriate ways, for there is no acceptance of poor behavior. From poor choices. He is learning responsibility for the choices he makes and knows he will have to deal with the consequences, such as heightened hyper-activity or sensory issues if he doesn't choose to refrain from eating something he shouldn't. He also knows eating gluten makes schooling more difficult as well as many other things that just isn't worth it. This has made a huge difference for him in learning self-control in all areas of life.

Everyone has felt a sense of reward and gratefulness for the time we each invested to help Richie recover, and he can reflect on how each member of our family has played an important part of each other's lives. Are we perfect? Definitely not! We're a human family living in a fallen world as sinners. We continue to grow and seek the Lord to overcome each challenge that presents itself every day. But when we fall we have promised to get up again. "A just man falls seven times and gets up again" (Proverbs 24:16a).

REFLECTIONS FOR RECOVERY

∞ Perhaps you have never considered homeschooling and this is the first you have even heard of the idea. If so, research your community to find support groups where you can gather more information to make a decision that might be right for your family.

∞ If homeschooling is not an option for you, research other methods and possibilities for your child and family. Be the best-educated advocate you can for your child and be involved in his life.

∞ Perhaps you are already in the midst of homeschooling, whether it was your choice from the beginning or your child just wasn't accepted or progressing at your local school. Whatever the case, it might not seem easy at times but it is so worth it. Hang in there and let down your expectations. Love and joy go a *long* way for teaching your special-needs child—any child.

∞ See appendix for homeschooling resources.

∞ Praise often! You can't praise your children enough. But be sure to praise their character, not their credentials or through flattery. Things that other children cannot achieve are not good to praise, like the blue eyes of one child when another has brown; those are unchangeable. Rather, praising one child's diligence in cleaning an area can inspire and encourage another to achieve the same praise. This will also encourage your children to become more concerned with their character over their credentials or physical image.

∞ Have you called upon others in your homeschooling community to help with your special-needs child so you can have the necessary time to school the others? This is a wonderful community outreach opportunity for others and a way to bless them.

∞ Our words can make such a difference—make your words count for character building!

∞ Many homeschooling young people would love the opportunity to learn how to play with and encourage your special-needs child. With a little instruction and guidance it might be a resource worth checking into.

∞ Is homeschooling the right choice? It's like anything else, you may not know unless you try it!

My Personal Thoughts

_____

_____

_____

PEARLS FOR OTHERS: "WHAT CAN I DO TO HELP?"

∞ Offer to watch children so parents can attend a homeschooling conference.

∞ Help be an advocate for a family in a public or private school system.

∞ Offer to be an aid once a week for a child in the school system or in a homeschool setting to help that child achieve his full potential.

∞ Offer to help with organizing, planning, making needed charts, etc. (See our Web site for more ideas.)

∞ Offer to research curriculum, purchase curriculum, or watch children monthly so a parent can do this planning and research.

∞ Offer to drive a special-needs child (or other children) to school to help with morning transitions.

∞ Praise the family often; any choice they make is going to have challenges. Parents and siblings need regular doses of encouragement.

Ways I Commit to Help Someone I Know

_____

_____

_____

"Train up a child in the way he should go and when he is old he shall not depart from it" (Proverbs 22:6).

REAPING REWARDS

Reverence:
Awareness of how God is working through
the people and events in my life to pro-
duce the character of Christ in me[9]

Once we began to see improvements in various areas of Richie's development, hidden challenges became new giants—those challenges obscured the progress we had made and then became the greater focus to dispose of for reaching recovery. It was like peeling an onion; layer after layer revealed yet another piece to peel. It seemed getting to the core was unforeseen. Therefore, keeping organized with the behavior and intervention charts, doctor records, menu and food eaten, etc., was immensely important to reflect where Richie had been and what had been accomplished. (See chart below.) Not losing sight of the immediate goals and looking too far ahead was equally important to continue making daily progress. Every bit forward counts, and every step backward is also valuable information. I had to view it that way to avoid discouragement or frustration. As the current tasks at hand seemed to be lacking progress and I even had a bit of doubt, I would retreat and review our past behavior charts, charts that I would nightly discipline myself to rate every behavior Richie was dealing with. On a scale of zero to nine I would rate how badly that behavior was to deal with each day, along with the interventions, therapies, and unusual occurrences. I could later reflect on how many nines we had in the beginning, and as we slowly slipped out of one difficult behavior into another, where we had come from. These charts were not only a useful tool to track interventions and better communicate results with our doctors and therapists, but they were also the inspiration God used that kept me going when I felt we weren't making progress. Upon reflection of those past charts, perspective was had, revealing all the symptoms that had been left behind but also forgotten, being readily replaced with the new giant we faced in our road to recovery. I have to admit even now, when I watch a video of autistic children I sit in awe with tears of remembrance of how that was our life and my son just a few short years ago. I never want to forget how hard it was so that I'll always feel a burden to help others just beginning in their struggles.

Behaviors / Date	Sun 10/3/04	Mon 10/4/04	Tue 10/5/04	Wed 10/6/04	Thu 10/7/04	Fri 10/8/04	Sat 10/9/04	Sun 10/10/04	Mon 10/11/04	Tue 10/12/04	Wed 10/13/04	Thu 10/14/04	Fri 10/15/04
Hyperactive													
Aggressive													
Loud voice													
Difficulty Transitioning													
Disobedience													
Inability to sit still at meals													
Sensory (Especially Skin)													
Stimming / Rubbing skin													
Pushing feet													
Frustration fits													
Resistant to doing chores													
Craving certain foods													
High pain threshold													
Acts of kindness													
Able to do things on his own													
Schooling - Ability to focus													

Meltdowns - Frequency												
Meltdowns - Severity												
Meltdowns - Duration												
Refuses Medication												
Biting his lips												
Headbanging / Punching												
Rubbing face / eyes												
Eczema (face / buttocks)												
Conversation (good)												
Notes:												
Unusual Circumstances												
Treatment Changes												

Sometimes when we are moving ahead we forget where we've come from. The troubles that lay ahead begin to tire us before we ever proceed. And that horizon seems ever before us, never accessible no matter how fast we run. We must just focus making continual daily progress, no matter what it is in life we are looking to achieve. If we don't, then all too often we will fall into the trap of procrastinating, feeling like we're too tired, like it won't matter, like we'll do it later or tomorrow. Proverb 26:13 says, "The slothful man saith, There is a lion in the way; a lion is in the streets." This reminds me of how our excuses can lead us into slothfulness. Once in that trap of procrastination quicksand it becomes hard to get out. However, no matter where you are at this moment, just commit to do one progressive action each day toward the goal to recovering your child, renewing a relationship, or reaching for a new goal. That will be your first step to recovery—not just from autism—but from procrastination. I have found that even if it's exercise and I have gotten out of a routine and now find it hard to make the time, if I just commit to anything, even five minutes of sit-ups, but do it daily, consistently, so will follow the desire and commitment to make that which is important gain back its rightful priority in my life. The quicker a decision is made and followed through, the sooner we will be on our way to reaching the horizon.

I once had a friend remind me that when you are weeding a garden it's much easier to nip those new minute fresh-grown weeds between your fingers, plucking out roots and all. However, the longer we leave those weeds to grow, the quicker, longer, and stronger those roots develop. If left too long, major tools are needed to remove them completely. We can't allow ourselves to grow lasting weeds in our life. Weeds of doubt, slothfulness, discouragement, procrastination, blame, anger, and the list goes on and can quickly take root if not dealt with expediently. Of course, we'll likely never be completely weed-free this side of heaven, but we can become a weeding expert by recognizing little sprouts as they arise, and plucking them out quickly and easily, grooming a beautiful garden of love within our hearts. I've found as long as I stay consistent in God's Word, I am convicted much more easily as I begin slipping into those traps. Then I can see the error of my ways, confess it, and change before those ugly weeds take deep root.

When you feel you're not progressing, review your past improvements. An additional way I tracked everything that was going on is by journaling daily. Though I did it during my morning prayer time and felt it was more of my way to express myself to the Lord and share struggles and praises with Him, it became an amazing way to go back and see how far we had come. Remembering is key to conquering discouragement. Discouragement, it has been said, is one of Satan's most readily used tools, for once he has you discouraged, he can get most anything he wants from you. First he'll steal your time and then your hope. Reflect on all that you do have; if it's still difficult, then continue to work at it one day at a time, even one moment at a time. Progress is just the continual advancement of doing the next priority.

I'll be ever grateful to a pastor we had early on who challenged our congregation to committing to beginning their day, no matter what time they would have to get up, with the Lord alone. For me having our fifth newborn, at that time, meant rising very early. But through these daily morning prayer and journaling times it became the source of strength that got me through each day. I know if I hadn't committed it first thing, prior to everyone waking as life with autism erected itself full swing, I never would have had a chance to spend quality time with the Lord during my days. And my nights always ended in total exhaustion. This morning devotional was a time where I poured my heart out, searched the Scriptures for at least one that I could take with me for the day, and only then did I feel I could tackle the new day's battles. This time was a diligent decision I had to make to rise before the rest of the family to begin my day in God's Word with prayer. Though it often meant less sleep, and having lupus, sleep was critical for me to avoid bad flares, God blessed the time and gave me all the strength I needed each day and I never experienced more symptoms with lupus it seemed; as long as I was faithful, I felt God's blessings.

I still treasure those early *alone* times to this day. Remember, you cannot eat an elephant in one bite! I encourage you to do what you can to commit to making God your first *meeting* of the morning. If you're not sure what to read, try reading the Proverb for the day. For example, on June first read Proverbs one, on the second read Proverbs two, and so on. This way you will read through the book of Proverbs each month. And there's much wisdom to glean through these readings, over and over again!

Reaping rewards will be your bonus when you don't grow weary in well doing. I often reflect on why certain phrases are in the Bible. And then as I go through life

God makes it clear to me—if we follow His words of wisdom, we will reap His rewards of promise. In the end we must revere the time we have. Life is so very short, and God has shown me to make the most of the time we have, the relationships we have—make the investment we need to live without regrets. Don't have exceedingly high expectations with recovery; don't think, *This one therapy or treatment will be the magic pill,* or you may set yourself up for discouragement and ultimately failure. I was almost there many times, holding on to one newly learned treatment or therapy as the last and final *cure all,* and I would put all my faith into one area, only to realize it helped, but our journey was not near over. I had to learn to focus on just doing the next thing. It takes work, effort, pain, yet then there's the promise of reaping the reward. Without all these ingredients you would miss the blessing of reward. It would not hold the same value if it were easy. All the character developed would be lost. That is what I have learned through this process of recovering our son. Though I wish it had been easier and less painful, I can now reflect on the beautiful colors of the rainbow those storms in my life produced. It's truly only the rainbows I most often reflect upon now.

Recovery Caution

One caution I must address is that recovery may not mean the same thing for each child. I talk often of recovery, as I feel that is where my son is for us—for him. It may not seem like it to some since he's still catching up academically, he is still on a special GFCF diet, and we do adjust certain activities based on that issue alone. But for us there is no comparison between where we were and where we are now. Richie will catch up in the few areas he needs to, and he is excelling in many other areas. He is a typical young boy who now has a whole life ahead of him with promise. He has great ideas for what he wants to be when he grows up. Just the other day he told me he still wants to be a construction worker (he loves all that big equipment) to earn his money and then he wants to be a therapist for children with autism for free. He said he could really help parents know what their child is thinking, and he could help the children know how to get better. This insight from him was so profound to me and meant so much to see him have a desire to help other children.

Perhaps you've been on the road to recovery for some time and are not experiencing many results. I was there for a time and through much prayer, God revealed many issues that needed addressing outside of autism. When they were taken care of, we began to see progress once more. I believe God allows things in our lives to teach and change us. Sometimes He then relieves us of a particular burden but sometimes He doesn't, and we must continue to persevere for Him and His glory. So it's then that I reflect that even Paul prayed three times for a thorn in the flesh to be removed. But God said, "My grace is sufficient for thee: for my strength is made perfect in weakness. Most gladly therefore will I rather glory in my infirmities, that the power of Christ may rest upon me" (II Corinthians 12:9). It's the second half of this verse that one day jumped out at me; I knew God's grace was sufficient for me and getting through those many tough days came from His strength. But to glory in my infirmities—gladly? That the power of Christ may rest upon me?

It is when that which I would love to be relieved from has become a glory for me to rest in the power of Christ to see me through each day that I realized even if that thorn in my flesh was autism not responding to any treatment I could rest on this same promise–His grace is sufficient. For me it's something different; for you it might be a child with autism not yet responding. Seek the Lord and then trust Him, His strength and His grace.

Brokenness

A final painful part of Richie's recovery was that I had to be broken myself before I could break the cycle of autism's inflicting pain. I had to let go of any and all anger, bitterness, envy, jealousy, regret; it all had to go. Until I was fully surrendered I could not really find the true joy and peace I now experience. When I didn't experience peace and joy was when I unknowingly harbored bitterness or anger because of how my son was damaged and the autism that resulted with all the ways our lives had been altered because of it. It was then that I lacked the inner peace and joy that was waiting for me. I don't believe I would have found that missing last piece to the puzzle if I hadn't confessed those feelings as the sin that they are and let go of them. I had to release them to God, who could totally dispose of them, so that I no longer had to be plagued with such destructive feelings.

Bitterness, anger, envy, jealousy are all some of the most damaging, destructive emotions we can experience. Consuming our thoughts, they will destroy our future for happiness. Our relationships will not survive. We'll totally miss out on improvements and perhaps taint all the efforts we make on our road to recovery. For me, once I totally gave it all back to the Lord, holding no regret, remorse, sorrow, sadness, or blame for the past; it was then that I was free to enjoy and recognize the recovery that had taken place. Richie's not perfect, nor am I, and we are now playing *catch up* in many areas of life. But I can do it all with peace, laughter, and joy with a heart of gratitude.

Isaiah 43:18–19 says, "Remember ye not the former things, neither consider the things of old. Behold, I will do a new thing; now it shall spring forth; shall ye not know it? I will even make a way in the wilderness, and rivers in the desert." Isaiah 55:8–9 states, "For my thoughts are not your thoughts, neither are your ways my ways, saith the Lord. For as the heavens are higher than the earth, so are my ways higher than your ways, and my thoughts than your thoughts." These verses have spoken boldly to me regarding where my focus needs to continually be. Not on the past, on what could have been, no room for what ifs—all that needs to be dropped. Let go. There are still many times I have to remind myself of these very verses and take my thoughts captive. But as I do, how wonderfully sweet is the flavor of the future.

REFLECTIONS FOR RECOVERY

∞ Are you willing to do what it takes for a season to give the blessing of reward to your family and child for a lifetime?

∞ Are you reaping the rewards of your efforts?

∞ If you're not, just reexamine what you're doing, if more could be done, if slothfulness has set in due to depression or pride in not seeking help, or whatever

God reveals to you, give it up to Him and move forward. You won't be sorry.

∞ Enjoy your family! Do what it takes to have some fun and laugh whenever you can. Autism can be funny at times! Send me your "funny autistic times," and I'll post them on our Web site for all to enjoy.

∞ Our funny! I recall a time when Richie was very young and nonverbal. A repairman came into our home, and while I was standing there talking with him, Richie crawled under my long skirt. The man did not see what had happened and I couldn't move without terrible embarrassment and concern for a meltdown with my son! Those few minutes seemed to last an eternity before he finally gave me the papers to sign and left. And that became the next "social training class" we did at home! Dresses are *not* tents! But now it's one of my reminiscent "funny" times!

∞ Sometimes you just have to laugh!

∞ If you've already been through divorce purpose to put any new insights you've received into all your relationships, including an ex-spouse, so that your children can reap the benefits of your integrity and character (love and forgiveness) by your example. Being broken and humble, forgiving and loving while taking all pride, anger, and bitterness and dumping those down the drain could be the best way to free yourself and those around you into a new and joyful life full of promise.

My Personal Thoughts

_____

_____

_____

PEARLS FOR OTHERS: "WHAT CAN I DO TO HELP?"

∞ Give grace and mercy. When a family, especially a stay-at-home mother, is dealing with autism on a 24/7 basis they might not make much since to you at times. Love them as Christ loves you and gently help them into balance.

∞ When you see self-condemnation, depression, withdrawal, or anything else negative, pray for and recognize this as a sign that this person needs help and love—even if they don't ask or even refuse it, pray how you might help.

∞ Rejoice in other's reaching recovery but realize it's never over for the family, for there are still possible dietary needs, supplements, and therapies necessary to maintain. Be there for the maintenance of the marriage and the recovery!

Ways I Commit to Help Someone I Know

_____

_____

_____

HAVING GRATITUDE

Gratefulness:
Making known to God and others in
what ways they have benefited my life[10]

A Grateful Heart

What good is recovery to any degree if our heart isn't right? We may have made improvements or even recovered our child from autism, but if we have just shifted what used to engulf our life with autism to another form of captivity—bitterness—what good will progress or recovery really be? Perhaps we'll free our child of the prison they're in but in the process hold ourselves captive in the prison of bitterness and unforgiveness. And be certain that if we harbor those feelings, they will undoubtedly be passed down to our innocent children. For me, as I was finally seeing progress with recovering my son from autism we were about to face yet another reality that I'm sure hits many families in our situation. An area that sought to induce bitterness, anger, and defeat—loss of finances.

Financial Strain

Everything was going better across the board—everything except our finances. I hadn't even realized the toll they had taken with all the investments of time and money to help bring our son to a place of recovery. Not only that, but add in the fact that my husband's business and political ambitions had been revoked almost overnight during autism's course of diagnosis and treatment, which left him without consistent income for a while. Couple that with continued efforts to treat Richie at that time and maintain our schooling schedule, the money was continuing to leave quicker than it was coming in. Rick had estimated spending out of pocket in excess of $200,000 to $300,000 on Richie's medical treatments, therapies, and dietary costs. Where were funds to continue to come from now? How could we possibly maintain what we had achieved in recovery? As for many people recovered from something, he still needed a special diet and a certain amount of supplements to maintain this state of recovery.

Walking by faith at this point became reality. We had already given up many of the conveniences we had previously appreciated with house cleaners, dry cleaners, lawn care, and house maintenance. We did it all, now. I did all Richie's therapies and the children and I added many other responsibilities to our already-busy schedule. Downsizing our home and cutting costs in every area was a way of life. We even sold a van after only having it a year to obtain funds during the time when there was no income. We now had to face another culprit of many family crises in our society. Finances. There was nothing left. There were no *extracurricular* activities to be afforded. Though many aspects of life had improved with our recovery process, there were certain maintenance expenses we needed to endure. Our grocery bill is substantial since we still maintain a gluten-free, casein-free menu not only for Richie, but along the road our fourth-born son was diagnosed with Celiac Disease, which meant he also had to be on the expensive gluten-free diet. There was obvious need for health insurance, housing, and some doctor maintenance care, so I continued to keep the focus on the end result, on the progress that had been made thus far by reviewing those past charts and at times my prayer journals, as they helped give perspective to where we had been, how much progress had been achieved, and the many prayers that were answered. Richie's recovery was now a reality, yet we still had to eat. We still had to maintain the necessities that required additional income.

We now faced this other side of the block. A side, until now, we had not had to completely experience. We were grateful to be able to transfer to another doctor as we relocated to Florida, Dr. Jeff Bradstreet, another leading doctor in treating autism and one whom we had been on a waiting list for had an opening. Since we ended up in the same town as his office, we no longer had to make expensive trips across the nation for Richie's appointments. So it made since to make that change. But at times, I found myself humbly explaining to him that we were too low on funds to even see him. We are so grateful to Dr. Bradstreet and ICDRC for keeping his focus on the well-being of our child's recovery throughout this season; because of that, he has helped us reach and maintain Richie's recovery process. He and his staff have been so loving and compassionate working with us and assisting us in any area we've needed. Dr. Bradstreet came with additional insight into treating autism, since he also has a son recovering. He was able to have that firsthand understanding of the 24/7 life with autism. Recognizing and acknowledging the financial toll for us was a blessing to our family, as he helped us sift through necessary tests/treatments while on our tight budget.

Our children at one point all qualified for Medicaid so if we had serious illness, they were at least covered. Learning to soak and cook raw beans, mashing them for our own bean dips and sauces, cooking whole grain rice, grinding rice and other GF grains for our flour, and changing our menu once again to exist on a very low-budget grocery bill while still maintaining the diet to continue with the special foods our sons needed brought us to new levels of humility. I gleaned much from other moms in how to maintain the specialized diets on such a tight budget. I recognized how blessed I was in the beginning to not have the financial strain during the height of Richie's autism when he needed so many interventions. Major paycheck-to-paycheck budgeting became a necessity. Although we could have changed many things—have me go back to work, put the kids in school—and made *finances* a priority, we proceeded cautiously in a focused effort not to undo all the progress we had made in so many areas. During this transition time I learned, more than ever, to be honest and humble about our situation to others. We sold cars, lived on borrowed money to pay our bills and groceries while we prayed for solutions.

It was during this time that God allowed in our lives I learned to reflect upon where we would be if we had not had an extra $300,000 in those early days to afford all of the many treatments, therapies, and foods we needed to bring Richie to recovery before the funds were gone. How many other children like Richie are not being recovered because insurance is not covering bills and they lack personal funds to afford treatment and therapy? This is when I developed a passion to support a nonprofit organization dedicated to provide funds to families for treatments and therapies not covered by insurance or available through other means than personal funds. A portion of the proceeds from this book will go into this fund for helping other children obtain the much-needed treatments and therapies.

I have to admit I much preferred to be on the other

side of the coin—the giver, not the receiver. Yet provision was made in every area. God gave us just what we needed when we needed it. Nothing more, nothing less. A box of clothes passed down from a friend, a bag of gluten-free groceries from our parents, there were many ways provision was made. I recall going *shopping* at the Goodwill store—this was hard—the first time I went with my husband, I left in tears. I had only ever dropped off donations, and now I needed to shop there—even finding things out of our budget there. But God was with us and was cultivating in us character and understanding in ways we could not have understood without having gone through this process of little to no income while accumulating unbelievable debt.

I have gained greater amounts of compassion and humility through all that we've been through. I would never again pass judgment on a parent who has a child throwing a tantrum in a store or park. I would sooner go and see if I could help, since I have no idea the reason behind the tantrum. If I see a family walk into Goodwill, rather I will lend a hand, smile, or prayer because I've been there. I know it wasn't because we were bad people or lazy people that we ended up where we did. It was because of a series of unfortunate circumstances—most of which were out of our control—and because we chose to put our family first instead of finances. The verse Paul writes to Philippians 4:11–13 is so prevalent, "Not that I speak in respect of want: for I have learned in whatsoever state I am therewith to be content. I know both how to be abased and I know how to abound: everywhere and in all things I am instructed both to be full and to be hungry, both to abound and to suffer need. I can do all things through Christ which strengtheneth me."

Giving Gratitude

Giving thanks and praise where it is due is vitally important. For me it was first to God, then family, doctors, therapists, friends, and especially my husband and children. Someone might look at you and say, "You did this! You recovered your child! You have such determination, strength, and energy..." But I have learned that when statements like those have been made and I might feel like saying, "You're right! I did invest, sacrifice, endure much," if I don't quickly transfer the focus away from myself, then I am setting myself up for the slippery slope into self-gratification. I realize that it really was never me, my strength, or even my determination. It was because of my faith in Christ, who has all the strength and grace offered to me. "And He said unto me, My grace is sufficient for thee: for my strength is made perfect in weakness. Most gladly therefore will I rather glory in my infirmities, that the power of Christ may rest upon me" (2 Corinthians 12:9). So, even if I did endure many aspects of my son's recovery without others here on earth, I can still recognize and deflect the focus away from myself and where it needs to go instead.

Besides, for me, it certainly wasn't *my* energy. I struggled with energy daily, sometimes moment by moment. I struggled with intense pain at times. Lupus wasn't easy to live with. I'm no super-mom. I'm just a plain, ordinary wife and mother who came to know the Lord, trusted Him for my strength, and then experienced many challenges in life. My hope and prayer is that I'm not the same person I was then. That I have become a softer, more pliable piece of clay offered up for continuous remolding. And I'm so grateful to others writings that inspired me along the way to endure.

Dr. D. James Kennedy writes, "Often when troubles come upon us we think God is destroying us. Actually, he is tuning us, like a harp. When you tune a harp, you must press it against your shoulder. Sometimes God presses us against his shoulder so that he might tune us, so that we might make more beautiful music for Him."[11]

I pray that the pressing I've experienced has helped me to make more beautiful music for Him. I know that my growing is not done. It will be a continual process until I die. But until that time, I pray that I can use all that God has allowed into my life and give back to others to help build hope for their own family's future, to hold a light during their darkness, and bring glory to God.

"In everything give thanks for this is the will of God in Christ Jesus concerning you" (1 Thessalonians 5:18).

REFLECTIONS FOR RECOVERY

∞ Do you have a humble heart?

∞ Or are you harboring resentment, bitterness, and anger toward your spouse, children, or other family and friends? What about toward those that you feel are responsible for causing your child's autism? You must let it go! Give it to God and allow Him to heal your pain.

∞ Do you feel that no one else can do things as good as you can? Or are you willing to accept help, even if it's not perfect or the way you would do it?

∞ Have you overdone your focus with research and

interventions where you have cut off others before hearing what they have to say?

∞ Have you examined and asked for input regarding the balance between your mission and your marriage?

∞ Do you have any amount of pride causing you to resist the help/advice of others?

∞ Are you plain wiped out and unable to see clearly? Do what you can to get support. Highlight the areas of this book that would help you and share it with someone who loves you. Or use it to help spark your own mind and jot down additional needs you have.

My Personal Thoughts

_____

_____

_____

PEARLS FOR OTHERS: "WHAT CAN I DO TO HELP?"

∞ Do you know a family struggling financially trying to help their child? Why not plan a fundraiser on their behalf? Have a bake sale, group yard sale…the possibilities are endless.

∞ If you're involved in a local organization, why not organize a "help day" to bless a family raising an autistic child—have a yard grooming day, flower planning day, painting day…

∞ Find out what a child's needs are, could they be helped by a special swing, bean bag, sand box, or some other type of resource? If so, why not get your local stores to help fund a "help a child" project by donating items needed, then plan to go and set up what needs to be.

∞ Don't think people are too proud for hand-me-downs! If there's an issue, why not drop them on the back porch when it's dark so you can bless the family in secret?

∞ A gift card to a local health food store or other online resource for GFCF foods would be a tremendous help to a child on that diet.

∞ The possibilities are endless, and if each person did just a small part, so many children and families would benefit.

∞ Remember, it's as much a blessing to give as to receive—a gift given in secret is best of all—you take away the need for guilt, writing a thank-you note, etc.!

Please note: Many families may be uncomfortable with anything major or public in means of fundraising; be sure to check with the family before pursuing something big that would not otherwise be anonymous.

Ways I Commit to Help Someone I Know

_____

_____

_____

"He that answereth a matter before he heareth it; it is folly and shame unto him" (Proverbs 18:13).

RECOVERING—OTHERS CAN HELP

Responsibility:
Knowing and doing what both God
and others are expecting from me[12]

Cultivate Care

Cultivating a caring attitude toward others who, in the past, condemned you and your efforts while letting go of all bitterness, anger, and strife, especially in the area of friends and family who may not have been well meaning during the season we embarked upon the great mission of recovering our child, took a decision. Dealing with criticism for the focus, dedication, intervention, strict diets, extreme financial investment, etc., is also an area of autism attack. Each person in this realm must lovingly forgive anyone who perhaps put a stumbling block in their road to recovery. Keep focused on the end result with a heart that remains right, then you'll likely live much longer to enjoy the benefits of your mission. It's a proven fact that anger, bitterness, and strife shorten a person's life. Ultimately, it's just not worth it. In the end you may find that your *own behavior* issues have developed you into a person others don't recognize. And you'll find it difficult to be happy, since you'll lack the ability to experience true joy. God tells us, "But now ye also put off all these; anger, wrath, malice, blasphemy, filthy communication out of your mouth" (Colossians 3:8).

Even if others do think you are crazy and wrong, if you love them along the way without allowing yourself to get off track then you'll have even more benefits in the end when your own child reaches the road to recovery and you have not severed relationships in the process. It's easy for us to think it's the others who are severing our relationships if we are having a self-righteous attitude. But ultimately we have the choice on how to proceed and if we want to do what it takes to keep our hearts and relationships with others right. I recall the verses in the Bible in which we are instructed to remove the plank from our own eye before we can remove the splinter from another's eye. It often doesn't appear that way at all in looking head on to a relational situation; however, I've come to realize it's often because that plank in our own eye is blocking the clear view. And with so many things in life, keep in mind that unless others walk the walk of raising/recovering a child with autism, they simply will not be able to truly understand all that we, who do, are going through. Receiving grace from others is as important as *us giving grace to others.* Colossians 4:6 says it best, "Let your speech be always with grace, seasoned with salt, that ye may know how ye ought to answer every man."

When my mother suffered with cancer and was going through treatments and recovery, as supportive, sympathetic, and loving as her family and friends were, when she got a call from a peer counselor—someone else who had already been exactly where she was, suffered the same form of cancer, and survived—there was an instant bond between the two of them that none of us could have. Since this woman felt the pain, personally experienced the emotions, fought the battle, and won, she was able to give my mother a connection that none of us could. It's the same with autism. Family and friends support is awesome, but having peer families who deal with autism daily will give a unique connection of understanding. If you haven't already done so, find other families walking the same walk or a support group if your area has one. If your area doesn't, consider starting a support group yourself. Then encourage each other! Families with autistic children all understand what life is like. There is a special and unique bond within communities that share a particular suffering. And if you use that connectedness to lift up and encourage each other through understanding, you'll find you can deal with all the other issues in life much better.

There are now many resources to be found online to help you know you're not alone in the war against autism. You'll find a resource list at the end of this book to help you begin the process. Though we may be tackling our own individual battles, there are many, many families waging war against autism. Together, with the help of the many doctors, therapists, and organizations researching for answers, this war can be conquered. And most importantly, our children can be healed.

One word of caution when seeking support: if a personal peer support helping you deal with autism becomes *too close* of a support, especially between members of the opposite sex, use caution and seek to find another source of support. Why? As we have already discovered autism not only attacks and seeks to destroy our children's abilities, it also attacks our marriages. Emotions are fragile for those of us in this battle. We all become tired and vulnerable at times. But in the process of supporting each other, if you begin violating marriage vows even with your mind or emotions, or find yourself in disrespectful communication regarding your own spouse, then your so-called *support* could really just end up deceptively destroying another aspect of your family. Flee and find another means of support. Sometimes it seems easier to get your emotional needs met by someone who understands but is also removed from your own intimate family and responsibility. But if this occurs, then there becomes another wedge for causing conflict in your life. Remember when you're walking through the desert (and autism can bring a family to the desert for a *long* time) then any mirage out there can look much more appealing to the eye and more thirst quenching than what's right before you. Use caution. Support needs to be for the *entire family's repair.*

Balance

On both sides of the coin balance needs to be reached. Generally speaking, the mother needs to not overdo and allow others to help, or seek out help if it doesn't just appear for her. She needs to be grateful to her spouse for anything he may contribute and yet not hold that person to unrealistic expectations, for this is where breakdowns can occur. She needs to not look down on others for their lack of understanding of her mission for her child or their lack of help in her areas of need or for their undue judgment of her child's behavior. She needs to be continually evaluating her mission and her life to keep things in balance. If something is lacking, if a relationship is being severed, most often with her husband or other children, then adjustment and repair needs to be the focal point for a time. Even if someone lacks in doing his part, we must focus on ours. Bringing balance with it all is a constant continuum. Like the pendulum of a clock, the swinging motion must be continually monitored so that it doesn't get off balance. Find out what your husband or other children need to feel loved and then commit to give it.

I believe the same holds true for husbands/fathers. Our children need your love, compassion, and patience.

We wives need your care, concern, and understanding. We need to feel loved and important, even if we get off balance for a time, which can be necessary in efforts to recover a child from autism. What better way to help us recognize and get back to swinging right than through our husband's love and support? Find out what your wife needs to feel loved and then seek to give it to her—especially now. Mothers need to feel loved, valued, and protected while they work hard recovering a child from autism. We need husbands who lift us up so II Corinthians 4:8–9 becomes our reality in a difficult situation. "We are troubled on every side, yet not distressed; we are perplexed, but not in despair; Persecuted, but not forsaken; cast down, but not destroyed." Christ ultimately holds us up but a loving supportive husband can transfer that love abundantly.

Though there are many times where major focus is necessary with recovering a child from autism or even taking on other challenges in life, and certain things must go as a result during a particularly challenging season. Sometimes we must make choices to give up certain activities we enjoy for a season. I had to give up my love for teaching ballet, running a ballet ministry that served many, and become very selective with activities that my other children participated in during a season of autism challenges. Guarding myself against comparison with other families who were doing things I simply couldn't was a constant challenge. No longer could I go on *play dates* with other families, nor have most any family over. Enjoyment with that sort of fellowship ended; between dietary challenges and behavior issues it was more than most people desired to deal with for a simple *get together* time. Although it hurt and isolation was painful, I had to admit that I never enjoyed myself much anywhere we went or while having others over or going places during those intense years. It was always a constant exhausting task keeping track of Richie, making sure he was okay and wasn't hurting himself, someone else, damaging property, or eating the wrong foods. I was also constantly intervening, trying to avoid breakdowns that could often occur because other children simply didn't understand what would set Richie off. I had to give up having *date nights* with my husband outside of our home for a time. We couldn't leave the children with a babysitter. Not many could handle five children plus autism, and those who tried usually didn't return. No one understood autism. They couldn't. We couldn't. We just survived doing the next thing. Instead, becoming creative in making date nights work within our home after bedtime was one small solution. Organizing fun-themed play times with my children was another. One sweet memory that developed during this time was having late night "tea parties" with my girls after the younger boys were asleep. We still enjoy these times to this day, as they've become a tradition for our mother daughter special times. I had to keep God the center of my days, taking every thought captive to avoid discouragement and continue with creativity.

At the end of life one rarely regrets activities they've not done with others but rather the relationships they neglected to nurture. Be it a spouse, children, extended family, or friends, regret comes when we've not taken the time and effort to invest properly into people. You must have a mission mind-set to accomplish the great task of recovering a child with autism; however, your mission must have balance in your life.

Be an Encourager

If you know anyone who is challenged with a special needs child, whether it's ADD, ADHD, autism, Asperger's, cerebral palsy, or anything else, encourage them to know that though it is hard, the growth through raising/working with their special needs child can far outweigh the defeat. When we are encouraging others it's impossible to be discouraged ourselves. Autism is not easy! *It's plain hard, discouraging, depressing, debilitating, and disheartening.* So you must come alongside and help them hold up their spirits. Even if you don't understand, you can still encourage. Even if you don't agree, you can still help. That is one of the reasons I have written this book and also included the "Reflections" and "Pearls for Others" at the end of each chapter, to give families insight into areas they could come alongside and support another family who is struggling.

My sister-in-law, who lived next door to us during many years of Richie's recovery, blessed me so many times by making special efforts to find out what Richie could eat at family/holiday functions and took care of that need for me. She and my brother-in-law, Phil, also often dropped off a bag of clothes for us. These were beautiful items that meant so much to me since our funds could not go to clothing purchases.

However, there were still many family and friends who did not initially understand autism or even accept that our son was truly inflicted with this dreaded disorder. Some even thought the medical interventions were fanatical and downright crazy. From their perspective I can't blame them, as I felt a bit fanatical myself at times seeking to heal our son. But when you live with the infliction of autism day in and day out, you become willing to do what you can to recover your child and bring normalcy back to your family. In time, many offered to help us attend family functions by fixing meals that our child could eat or asked for ways they could help. How extremely grateful I am to all of our extended family and friends for their love and support along the way. You can become clouded by negatives or you can choose to be grateful for any positive. And you can find positive in almost any situation or person if you truly seek it. Warning: you must get rid of any pride/bitterness, or else those items will work like a blindfold, making it so you can no longer see the good. It's like that age-old cliché of a half-filled cup of water. Do you see it as half empty or half full? You can *choose* to see it half full if you work at it and make the choice.

As I was writing this part of this book, I had two sick children and was sitting next to them typing away editing, rewording, and adding paragraphs. After about three and a half hours of work I finally completed the book to where I was going to be finished. I carefully saved my work and even backed it up on the flash drive I have. (I've always been paranoid of losing something and having to recreate it because my time is so limited that having to recreate the *time* seems as much of a task as the words!) The next morning as I opened up my file to add one final quote, I noticed that some items I had changed the night before were no longer there. As panic set in I sought the technical expertise of my husband. I specifically remembered when I saved my book to my stick, the time about 2:30 a.m. and size of the file I was replacing. However, after a few hours of searching, it was simply not to be found. Nothing was saved past 11:00 p.m. the night before on either device. I then had to look at that cup and see it as half full and consider that perhaps there was something different I needed to redo on those forty plus pages. Back to trying to find a quiet moment to recreate the work. To this day, it's a mystery. Simply no explanation for why both files did not save. So I just chalked it up to another *hug* from the Lord, allowing me to live out what I was writing and to His Glory, I didn't get upset; instead I just sat down to recreate my work. So this book and these words have impacted my heart as I write them to make a difference, and I hope they'll do the same for you.

Reflections for Recovery

∞ Are there too many things on your plate while you are seeking to help your child recover? Or do you simply need to drop some activities?

∞ Are you able to balance time with your spouse, your special-needs child, and your other children?

∞ Have you joined a support group to glean insight and encouragement as you run the race to recovery?

∞ Are you content where you are or feeling left out, comparing your family to others? Look within your home to discover the gems inside your spouse and children. Love them all. And remember:

"And we know that all things work together for good to them that love God, to them who are called according to His purpose"

(Romans 8:28).

My Personal Thoughts

_____

_____

_____

Pearls for Others: "What can I do to help?"

We've covered ideas pertaining to specific areas at the close of each chapter. Below is an list, certainly not exhaustive of what you could do, but to just ignite the fire inside of you to begin giving you ideas of the many ways others can come alongside the many families afflicted with autism and make a difference. Know that when you help a child, you help a family, a community, a nation, a world. You have no idea what impact you might make. Don't wait; procrastination prevents progress. Time won't wait. Choose something to do today!

∞ Research for them.

∞ Take them to doctor, therapy appointments—take notes, tape record (with permission), video tape.

∞ Shop for groceries or other items they may need for their child that are hard to find.

∞ Take their other children out for fun times during therapy, doctor appointments.

∞ Take their special-needs child with you so the family can do "typical" family outings together.

∞ Fix large mixes/foods that are easy to prepare or able to freeze for quick meals—especially important if on a special diet.

∞ Research restaurants they can go to.

- ∞ Research/help obtain state funding.
- ∞ Make insurance phone calls.
- ∞ Clean their house.
- ∞ Organize their house.
- ∞ Plant flowers for them.
- ∞ Plant a garden for them.
- ∞ Paint a room.
- ∞ Take them on vacation (and don't correct their "special" child).
- ∞ Bring meals over (especially on therapy days).
- ∞ Learn and help with in-home therapy.
- ∞ Make cassette tapes of affirmations for family and special-needs child.
- ∞ Send notes of encouragement.
- ∞ Bring a puppy to play for a day.
- ∞ Take the family swimming.
- ∞ Do their ironing.
- ∞ Do their laundry.
- ∞ Help teach their children these things.
- ∞ Love them.
- ∞ Pray with them and for them—often!

Ways I Commit to Help Someone I Know

_____

_____

_____

CULMINATING COUNTLESS EFFORTS

Contentment:
Realizing that God has provided every-
thing I need for my present happiness

Keeping a Clean Heart

As you go through this process yourself and make inroads with your family, be certain that your heart doesn't get muddy along the way. It's important to stop and take as many heart washes as necessary to keep the mud clear from clogging any arteries that lead into our hearts. The main clogging culprits I see (and must admit I experienced myself at times) were dealing with pride (look what I did for my family, how much I sacrificed), there was bitterness (my life isn't anything I thought it would be—we might be better in many ways, but where are we going to end up now? There were also moments of anger (autism stole the best years of my life; my child is better, but what about me? I'm worn and aged). At that point I thought, we're broke, in debt, our children are growing older, how can we even think of college or weddings? I know we're not alone in this battle that autism takes on family's finances. I know many others who have experienced the same kinds of struggles or worse. But trusting the Lord with the future has been an ongoing place I've been; before it was with autism and recovery, now with finances. God has been faithful in providing resources, new opportunities, and as always, hope for the future. It didn't come quickly, not in our timing, but it is coming in God's timing.

The way I had to tackle those unhealthy heart killers was through humbling myself and truly being broken over those harmfully wrong feelings. Reflecting on the sacrifices that Christ made on my behalf is still the constant forefront of my mind. I am grateful to have only allowed those destroyer thoughts to quickly flicker through, disposing of them and then moving forward, picking up my cross daily and recognizing nothing I've been through can compare to what Christ did for me at Calvary. Knowing that He has been where I am, He has had to deal with unfair judgment, self-sacrifice, pain, and suffering, greater than I could ever imagine convinces me that He understands when I cry out to Him with all that I am dealing with. His promise to never leave me nor forsake me has seen me through many days. Again, I believe, though I didn't always recognize it at the time, that the example of my parents and my in-laws reflected in me that I could *choose* how I wanted to view these things in life and either use them for positive progress or allow them to rot and harden my heart. Going to Christ and surrendering all those *justified* feelings to Him got me over the hump. But I have to go to Him daily—first thing in the morning—before anything else can distract me to gain wisdom. As Proverbs 8:17 says, "I love them that love me; and those that seek me early shall find me."

I am grateful to be able to go to God and confess those wrong feelings, knowing that I have been forgiven. It's been through going repeatedly back to the Lord that I have regained strength to continue pushing forward. It is my heart's desire to encourage you to not fall into those same destructive traps and if you do, like I have, get out quickly before roots are taken and begin to grow deep into your heart.

I believe in life we will all encounter many opportunities to choose either positive, God-honoring responses or destructive ones. I'm grateful for God's Word and for many other resources from people who help others to choose proper attitudes.

Looking at each new challenge in life as a new adventure rather than a new crisis has made the difference for me. When difficult things happen, and they will to all of us, we can choose to allow those *circumstances* to control our destiny, or we can make the *choice* to have them cultivate greater character within. Each of us has room to grow in various areas, and if we think, *Not me,* then I would consider examining our heart for pride. Like the story of the prodigal son who obviously sinned greatly, yet upon his return home after repenting and having a changed heart, he was no longer the prodigal. For he had been renewed and changed, forgiven of his sin, but now sin revealed itself in his older, righteous brother. The one who did right on the outside, looked good until the day of rejoicing came for his younger, sinful yet repentant, forgiven, and changed brother. As everyone else rejoiced at the party, this eldest son, who had that same "not me" attitude, was unable to accept that he also needed a repentant heart. It's the only way to have love and forgiveness for others. The only way to beat bitterness. Instead, he ended up the only one *outside* of the party and celebration. When we confess our sins, then He is faithful and just to forgive us our sins. Life is too short—like a vapor—to waste even a moment of it with bitterness, pride, or anger. Once we totally give it up and allow a broken heart to bestow a humble heart, then we'll experience joy and blessing like we can't imagine. "The sacrifices of God are a broken spirit; a broken and contrite heart, O God, thou wilt not despise" (Psalm 51:17).

Contentment in Your Heart

There are many ways that we can think we are being content in our hearts, yet when we truly examine them we find that we are actually operating out of discontentment. I once heard a tale of a man who was a stonebreaker and was working by the side of the road when he saw a lord riding grandly by. Immediately the stonebreaker wished that he were a lord. So a fairy instantly gave him his desire. But he had not long been a lord when he saw a king riding in great grandeur. So he wished he were a king. Again, his request was granted. But one day, as his majesty was thinking about the immense force controlled by the sun, he caught himself wishing that he were the sun! He then would have the great planets at his mercy. Again, his desire was granted and he was changed.

But one day, as he was shining in his strength, a cloud came between him and the spot on which he wished to focus his burning ray. "I wish," he cried, "that I were a cloud, able to defy the sun!" A cloud he at once became. But as, in his new capacity, he was one day flooding the earth and laughing over its swollen torrents, he saw one huge rock that proudly defied the swirling waters. "I wish," he exclaimed, "I had a hammer and could smash that rock in pieces!" And in a moment he found himself sitting beside the heap of granite by the roadside with a hammer in his hand.

This tale tells how much we all could go around changing many things in our lives, wishing always something were different or we were a different person in a different place, yet in the end I believe God has us right where it is best for us to be. It may not be a perfect scenario. It may seem unfair. But Christ Himself came down from His glory in heaven to live in an unfair world, in a poor, despised community. Even His own people rejected Him. Life wasn't fair for Him here on earth, and we shouldn't expect it to be for us either while we are here. Life isn't about fairness. It's about taking what we have and giving back to a God who is in control. Who is sovereign. Who does love us and cares for us. Who is our strength, our protector, our counselor, our everything—if we allow Him to be. When we do, that is when we can be content with where we are this very minute in life. This is when we can find joy, peace and contentment.

I know because I've experienced both sides of this block. I can walk through the grocery store every week and despise shopping because my funds are tight, yet I still have to shop gluten and casein free. Just trying to get food within our budget is a weekly chore. Walking up and down the grocery aisles wishing I could just pick up a sale loaf of bread and a bag of lunch meat for sandwiches for the week is something I have to guard myself against. I must always keep focused on how great good health is and what might seem a sacrifice really is a blessing. I can desire things in my life to be different, always seeking to change certain things, be like other people I know who seem to have an easier life in a particular area, or I can choose to become content in where God has me and wait on Him, trusting Him with my future. This is when I experience total peace and contentment.

Growing a Garden

Growing a garden of thanks and continual praise is not only possible but absolutely essential. When we continue to *choose* to look at everything and everyone through an eye for gratitude and praise we will become happier, more joy-filled people. For me, it's been my choice, and I'm grateful to have learned that key to happiness: not allowing my circumstances to determine my state of mind. My heart's desire is focused upon gathering others to help encourage, educate, and equip them for their own success. Sometimes we just assume family and friends should trust us, believe us, and know what we are talking about and how we are feeling. But there are times when that is not the case, nor should it be. A lesson I've learned: never think the worst, never assume others understand you recognizing your needs, and never become offended. Be content where you are, but work toward a greater future.

REFLECTIONS FOR OTHERS

∞ Is there anyone you need to forgive? Be sure to ask God to show you. He has a way of bringing people to mind when we ask, then we must truly forgive others and not allow past hurts to control us today or in the future.

∞ Is there anyone you've offended, hurt, or in some way requires an apology? If so, be quick to go and apologize, the way that will make them know that you are truly sorry.

∞ Do you believe that your life, marriage, and family could be better? Do you trust God's Word and believe it to be true? Are you willing to do what it takes, to change, sacrifice, forgive, and apologize to your spouse, children, family, friends, doctors, thera-

pists, strangers, pharmaceutical companies, and anyone else you may have a grudge against?
- ∞ Analyze if you are truly content, and if you're not, go to God and allow Him to reveal those reasons for discontentment and then purpose to change.

My Personal Thoughts

PEARLS FOR OTHERS: "WHAT CAN I DO TO HELP?"

- ∞ Do you see a family that is struggling? Take the children for a regular time for the parents to have an uninterrupted night alone. If you can, commit to a consistent time they can rely on.
- ∞ Commit to pray for a family, for their marriage, children, and their needs (see appendix).
- ∞ Do you know a family who struggles with finances or with the foods their children can eat? Be careful not to hurt that family accidentally when talking about what you do or where you eat. For that matter, be careful what you complain about to others. I once had a friend complain that on her budget she had to continually feed her children peanut butter and jelly on cheap bread; I thought if only I had it that easy! My children would love peanut butter and jelly on any bread!
- ∞ We are all in different places at different points. If you notice that a family doesn't participate in church

activities, why not inquire why rather than come up with assumptions. I often couldn't participate in many activities since food was always given and I couldn't control what my child was given to eat. Being sensitive to these types of needs can make a world of difference to a family. It is often not difficult to change a candy reward to a little trinket reward.

∞ Get creative on how you can help a family participate in activities within your church or circle of friends so during this recovery process or for those who have recovered but maintain a special diet, they have a friend who steps up to make this area of life a little easier.

Ways I Commit to Help Someone I Know

_____

_____

_____

JOY FOR LIFE

Joyfulness:
The spontaneous enthusiasm of my spirit
when my soul is in fellowship with the Lord

J. O. Y.

Where are you? Are you filled with joy despite what is going on around you? Or have you fallen into the why me (my child, my family, my marriage) self-pity syndrome? I've been there and asked those questions myself, I think we all have at some point in our life. But the key is to not go past a flickering thought. I had a friend not long ago diagnosed with a brain tumor. She died soon after her diagnosis. At her funeral, there were signs of J.O.Y. everywhere. During the service her pastor explained that Sharon had those words on every shape and size around her home to remind her how to live. And he went on to explain how her life exemplified the meaning of those words. He then explained the meaning: J stands for Jesus, put him first in your life; O stands for Others, put others next; and Y stands for Yourself, last. As I reflected I could clearly see J.O.Y. lived out in her life as I knew her. I now have that word J.O.Y. around me often, reminding me the way to continue experiencing J.O.Y. in my life is by keeping my life in that order.

Wherever you are right now, you can choose to continue; just begin to press forward, taking one step at a time, even if they're baby steps, rejoicing in whatever progress you make. And if you don't make any, at least you've made a step somewhere and you know where not to go. Everything can lead to something. Each step in the great masterpiece of autism is another piece to the puzzle—a piece that either fits into your child's complete picture or one that you know you do not need. Either way you win, since you've discovered something important. Keeping this focus allowed me to stay out of the unproductive pits that, if I would slip in, seemed to devour my family and me. If you're in a pit, just begin small, take the next step, and rise above. Through prayer and faith you can do it! It's never been through my own strength, but rather through the strength of Christ in me. And His strength is available to all of us who seek it.

The most important thing is not to lose hope. For when you lose hope you begin to die. When you begin to die, those around you begin to die too. When you all die, you rot. And when you rot, it begins to smell bad, really bad. If you get to that point, then it will be harder to get cleaned up and begin to grow again. But, remember, with Christ all things are possible. Even if you feel you are rotting away right now with all the many pressures before you—God can restore. Do not doubt Him. "All things work together for good to those who love Him to those who are called according to His purpose" (Romans 8:28).

I once had a dear friend tell me that if I am discouraged or doubting then I am calling God a liar, for He says He will take care of me and work all things for my good. I didn't like to hear that because I battled discouragement daily at times. Believe me, there were many times I wondered how any good could come out of all we were going through. The waters were very deep. But I now see the lessons I've learned, the character that's been instilled in my family and me, and the faith that I've grown through this process. For all of us, the process is still in progress. We are a continual work. Do I feel we've arrived? Hardly! We're just beginning. But we have experienced the many blessings from choosing to do things God's way. And I'm so excited to see what's ahead!

Perhaps you've had a rough start like we've had; perhaps you started running only to fall; perhaps you're down now, if so remember this, "For a just man falls seven times, and rises up again" (Proverbs 24:16a, NKJV). If you've fallen, or you do fall in the future, remember to get back up! Grab a hold of the hand of God. He promises never to leave you nor forsake you. That is something worth hanging on to. When you don't know what the future holds, He does. He knows and He cares deeply for you.

I once heard a poem by D.H. Groberg many years ago. I always liked the following version. Little did I know how impacting that poem would be. I obtained a copy and have used it in years past to share with and encourage others. It has been a huge source of encouragement for me and for my son, as I helped him achieve various strides in his recovery. I hope it will stay with you as it has me—becoming a reflection of finishing the race—for me it was Richie's Race.

The Race

"*Quit! Give up! You're beaten!*" They shout and plead, There's just too much against you now, this time you can't succeed.

And as I start to hang my head in front of failure's face,

My downward fall is broken by the memory of a race.

And hope refills my weakened will as I recall that scene.

For just the thought of that short race rejuvenates my being.

A children's race, young boys, young men; now I remember well.

Excitement, sure, but also fear; it wasn't hard to tell.

They all lined up so full of hope. Each thought to win that race.

Or tie for first, or if not that, at least take second place.

And fathers watched from off the side, each cheering for his son.

And each boy hoped to show his dad that he would be the one.

The whistle blew and off they went, young hearts and hopes of fire.

To win, to be the hero there, was each young boy's desire.

And one boy in particular, his dad was in the crowd,

Was running near the lead and thought, "My

dad will be so proud."

But as he speeded down the field across a shal-
low dip,

The little boy who thought to win, lost his step
and slipped.

Trying hard to catch himself, his hands flew out
to brace,

And mid the laughter of the crowd, he fell flat
on his face.

So down he fell and with him hope. He
couldn't win it now.

Embarrassed, sad, he only wished to disappear
somehow.

But as he fell, his dad stood up and showed his
anxious face,

Which to the boy so clearly said, "Get up and
win that race!"

He quickly rose, no damage done—behind a
bit, that's all,

And ran with all his mind and might to make
up for his fall.

So anxious to restore himself to catch up and
to win,

His mind went faster than his legs. He slipped
and fell again.

He wished that he had quit before with only
one disgrace.

I'm hopeless as a runner now, I shouldn't try to
race.

But, in the laughing crowd he searched and
found his father's face

That steady look that said again, "Get up and

win the race."

So, he jumped up to try again. Ten yards behind the last.

If I'm to gain those yards, he thought, *I've got to run real fast.*

Exceeding everything he had, he regained eight or ten,

But trying so hard to catch the lead, he slipped and fell again.

Defeat! He lay there silently, a tear dropped from his eye.

There's no sense running anymore—three strikes and I'm out—why try?

The will to rise had disappeared, all hope had flown away.

So far behind, so error prone, closer all the way.

I've lost, so what's the use, he thought, *I'll live with my disgrace.*

But then he thought about his dad, who soon he'd have to face.

"Get up," an echo sounded low. "Get up and take your place.

You were not meant for failure here, get up and win the race."

With borrowed will, "Get up," it said, "You haven't lost at all,

For winning is not more than this, to rise each time you fall."

So up he rose to win once more. And with a new commit,

He resolved that win or lose, at least he wouldn't quit.

So far behind the others now, the most he'd
ever been.

Still he gave it all he had and ran as though to
win.

Three times he'd fallen stumbling, three times
he'd rose again.

Too far behind to hope to win, he still ran to
the end.

They cheered the winning runner as he crossed
first place.

Head high and proud and happy; no falling, no
disgrace.

But when the fallen youngster crossed the line,
last place,

The crowd gave him the greater cheer for finishing the race.

And even though he came in last, with head
bowed low, unproud;

You would have thought he'd won the race, to
listen to the crowd.

And to his dad he sadly said, "I didn't do so
well."

"To me you won," his father said. "You rose
each time you fell."

And when things seemed dark and hard and
difficult to face,

The memory of that little boy—helps me in my
race.

For all of life is like that race, with ups and
down and all,

And all you have to do to win—is rise each
time you fall.

"*Quit!*" "*Give up, you're beaten.*" They still shout
in my face.
But another voice within me says,
"*Get up and win the race!*"

Have you had success recovering your child or just
making progress? If so, I want to hear from you! E-mail
me at kristi@kristichrysler.com and we will post your
listings so that others have a place to go for encouragement, hope, and motivation to stay on the course.

APPENDIX

Heaven and Christian Life

www.iblp.org
www.eeinternational.org
www.pcanet.org
http://everystudent.com/features/gettingconnected.html

Marriage

www.marriagebuilders.com

Autism

www.kristichrysler.com
www.autismresearchinstitute.org
www.autismone.org
www.autisminfo.org
www.tacanow.org
www.icdrc.org
www.immunolabs.com
www.childrenofdestiny.org
www.gfcf.com

Homeschooling

www.hslda.org

ENDNOTES

1   DeMoss, Nancy Leigh. *Surrender The Heart God Controls.* Moody Publishing, 2005.

2   Joni and Friends Daily Devotional E-Mail, May 3, 2007.

3   "Operational Definitions of Character Qualities," used by permission from IBLP, *Character Clues* 1981.

4   "Operational Definitions of Character Qualities," used by permission from IBLP, *Character Clues* 1981.

5   "Operational Definitions of Character Qualities," used by permission from IBLP, *Character Clues* 1981.

6   "Operational Definitions of Character Qualities," used by permission from IBLP, *Character Clues* 1981.

7   "Operational Definitions of Character Qualities," used by permission from IBLP, *Character Clues* 1981.

8   "Operational Definitions of Character Qualities," used by permission from IBLP, *Character Clues* 1981.

9   "Operational Definitions of Character Qualities," used by permission from IBLP, *Character Clues* 1981.

10   "Operational Definitions of Character Qualities,"
       used by permission from IBLP, *Character Clues* 1981.

11   Kennedy, Dr. James D. *Turn it to Gold.* Servant Pub-
       lications, 1991.

12   "Operational Definitions of Character Qualities,"
       used by permission from IBLP, *Character Clues* 1981.